BERKSHIRE

Edited by Dave Thomas

First published in Great Britain in 1999 by
POETRY NOW YOUNG WRITERS
Remus House,
Coltsfoot Drive,
Woodston,
Peterborough, PE2 9JX
Telephone (01733) 890066

HB ISBN 075431 514 2
SB ISBN 075431 515 0

FOREWORD

Poetry Now Young Writers have produced poetry books in conjunction with schools for over eight years; providing a platform for talented young people to shine. This year, the Celebration 2000 collection of regional anthologies were developed with the millennium in mind.

With the nation taking stock of how far we have come, and reflecting on what we want to achieve in the future, our anthologies give a vivid insight into the thoughts and experiences of the younger generation.

We were once again impressed with the quality and attention to detail of every entry received and hope you will enjoy the poems we have decided to feature in *Celebration 2000 Berkshire* for many years to come.

CONTENTS

James Mooney	57
Alastair Sharpe	58
Rebecca Taylor	58
Andy Owens	59
Ben Thorpe	59
Tony Barker	60
Liam Tomkins	60
Christopher Black	61
Lucy Bristow	61
Rachel Simpson	62
Stephanie Waters	62
Nicky Woodward	63
Isabel Somerville Baddeley	63
Amy-Lee Paradise	64
Adam Smiter	64
Neha Sharma	65
Sunita Patel	66
Callum Hall	66
Helen May-Bowles	67
Ben Allen	67
Anna Coles	68
Michael Irving	69
Rebecca Chappell	70
Joanne Bradley	70
Nicola Schwiezer	71
Hannah Smiter	71
Ben Canning	72
James Thomas	72
Carly Sansom	73
Tom Sturley	73

Sandy Lane Junior School

Sasha Peterson	74
Fiona Churchman	74
Charlotte Oram	74
Dale Nelson	75
Sam Viccars	75
Nathan Emmerson	76

Emma Dixon	115
Kimberley Sage	115
Megan Warman	116
Natasha Singh	116
Graham Newell	117
William Croxford	118
Rhys Bevan	118
Sarah Taylor	119
Danny Bungay	120
Nikki Perry	120
Charlotte Knibbs	121
Samuel Hughes	121
Hannah Myers	122
Megan Holgate	122
Emily Bryant	123
Ben Knight	123
Joanna Martin	124
Kandice Roberts	124
Alexander Richards	124
Clara Ramsdale	125
Luke Metcalfe	125
Chelsea Henderson	126
Emma Shoubridge	126
Emma Lobar	127
Rebecca Comerford	127
Carla Mackay	128
Rebecca Halfacre	128
Chloe Collins	129
Leisha-Louise Hann	129
Emma Pugh	130
Sam Dennis	130
Vincenza Stevens	131
David Nicholls	131
Emily Hanbury	132
Stefan Goniszewski	133

Shinfield St Mary's School

Kimberley Slark	133

The Poems

JOURNEYS

Journeys are good
Journeys are fun
Sitting still gives me a pain in the bum
I start fidgeting, my legs are stiff
I start asking for food like crisps
Mum says 'Play a game, you can't be hungry,
You have just eaten
You can't be hungry again.'
I ask my brother to play a game but he is just
Moaning because he wanted to go by plane.
So now I am bored with nothing to do
And all of a sudden I need the loo.
Dad's not happy as you can guess
We stopped a few miles back and had a rest.

Nicola Terry (11)
Aldermaston CE Primary School

MUM AND DAD

My mum and dad are so cool
My dad goes to work
And my mum takes me to school
In the summer we go to the swimming pool
Because we need to keep very cool.

I really love my mum and dad,
They're so kind and they keep me from being sad
They're quite strict but they're never that bad
My mum and dad are so cool
My dad goes to work
And my mum takes me to school.

Anna Powers (9)
Aldermaston CE Primary School

THE DEATH OF A CARROT

'Don't pull me by the hair,' he said
As I pulled him from the ground.
'Don't wreck my little orange head,'
He said with quite a sound.

He is now in his grave,
Down far in my tummy.
I've got a terrible crave,
But I enjoyed eating him, he was yummy.

I do feel sorry for him you know,
He didn't have a joyful life.
But now I have to move on and go . . .
I chopped him up with a carving knife.

Carly Mitchell (11)
Aldermaston CE Primary School

THE DEATH OF AN ONION

Ouch! The onion goes as it gets pulled out of the ground
It makes a rumbling crying sound.
It makes me cry as if to say 'Don't peel me, I'll cry'
When I cook the onion, it says to me 'Don't cook me, I'll die.'

In my stomach is its grave
It is dark and scary like a cave,
It lies there without a sound
Not moving at all on the ground.

Stephanie Kent (10)
Aldermaston CE Primary School

THE DEATH OF MY POTATO

My poor old potato died last night,
He was sitting on the window sill,
Oh I did get a fright!

He served me well,
And gave me delicious chips,
Oh, I would never sell!

But now at least he is at peace,
Hopefully not in the section,
With the beef!

He had a good life,
But now I can only have his friend's chips,
And they're probably with the baloney!

Samantha Taylor (10)
Aldermaston CE Primary School

CATS

Some cats are cool,
Some cats are fat,
Some cats are fuzzy,
And some cats are
Cats!

So if you have a cat
In your house,
Then you'll find that
You won't have a mouse.

Harriet Joy (10)
Aldermaston CE Primary School

THE DEATH OF THE PEA

They were round, smooth and yummy,
But now alas they've gone,
They're now in my tummy,
They haven't been there long.

They didn't want to be eaten so
They stayed in groups on my plate,
Were they OK? No!
Unfortunately they were too late.

There they lie, inside myself,
Alas, I am ashamed
As they were in good health,
I fear I am to blame.

I shouldn't have eaten those 40 peas,
I'm so, so sad,
But can I have some more please
Even though I'm really bad?

I am a rusty grave,
For peas, and peas alike,
I have a horrid crave,
The peas, they took a hike!

Chloe Cane (10)
Aldermaston CE Primary School

THE DEATH OF A PEA

This is the story
Of the death of a pea
Who sadly died
When flicked by me.

A baby licked it
It rolled on the floor
My brother kicked it
It went out the door.

It rolled on the grass
But only just
It hit a pane of glass
And turned into dust.

Nicky Prouse (10)
Aldermaston CE Primary School

CONCERT

With the drum going
Bang! . . . Bang! . . . Crash! . . . Crash!
Humongous sounds of the tuba
The *ting ting* of the teeny-weeny
triangle
Hear them coming
Hear the band
The gold gleaming shiny trumpet in
the band
Hear them coming
Hear the band.

Conor Reeves (6)
Binfield CE Primary School

AT NIGHT

I go to bed
The brilliant moon
Outside in the distance,
The gleaming stars in the sky,
I hear the TV downstairs in the lounge,
Laughing as jokes get told
To their friends on the settee
Next to them.
As the jokes get passed on, on, on,
I go to bed,
I see the gleaming stars,
The shining moon,
The dogs *howling,*
Cats *miaowing,*
Foxes *growling,*
Looking for their food in every bin.
I go to bed.

Matthew Donaldson (6)
Binfield CE Primary School

CHRISTMAS MEANS TO ME

Christmas means to me neatly wrapped presents,
Christmas means to me Christmas trees
very well decorated,
Christmas means to me Christmas pudding
bursting with chocolate sauce,
Christmas means to me gold shiny silver toys,
Christmas means to me roasted turkey smelling
in the oven, I can't wait to taste it,
Christmas means to me Jesus who was a special baby.

Thomas Gillham (7)
Binfield CE Primary School

MY WASHDAY

Every morning I get up
And put my clothes on
And go downstairs
I get a big shiny bowl from the cupboard
I fill it with some warm soapy water
I take it to the garden
Scrub, scrub, scrub, goes the washboard.
I dunk the dirty clothes in the clean water
I put some slippery green shiny soap on
Scrub, scrub, scrub, goes the washboard.
Wash it all off
Put it in the mangle
And squeeze all the water out.
Scrub, scrub, scrub, goes the washboard.

Fiona Bovis (7)
Binfield CE Primary School

OUR CONCERT

Crash! Bang!
Here comes the band
Gleaming shiny gold trumpet
The roof is going to come off
The racket of the band
Listen to the racket of the band
And listen to the beat of the trombone
Boom! Boom! Boom!
Here comes the band
The band is here.

James Board (6)
Binfield CE Primary School

NIGHT THOUGHTS

When I am looking through my window
I see . . . the dark dusty night
The rustle of the bush
The tick of the clock
The shimmer of the light.
When I am looking through my window
I see . . . the beautiful glinting orange sunset
And the brown striped bushy-feathered owl that
Hooted
And tried to keep me up all night.
I'm weary, I'm weary.
When I am looking through my window
I see the glistening moon looking at me
And the different colours emerging.
The noise is getting slower and slower
I hear the green mower
I hear the green mower.
Then I *s i n k* down into my bed.

Emily Drablow (7)
Binfield CE Primary School

HAPPINESS IS, SADNESS IS

Happiness is reading magic faraway
stories on my own.
Happiness is when I get my certificate in
Assembly
And standing, looking, staring, at people.
Happiness is when Daddy comes home from
Stockport in Manchester
That is a long way off
Happiness is when Daddy reads me and
Lewis a nice calm story before bedtime.

Sadness is when Daddy is away
When he is in Stockport all alone
in his room.
Sadness is when Mummy shouts at me.
Sadness is playing on a rainy day
all on my own, alone.
Sadness is when people hurt me.
Sadness is when I have nobody to play with.

Megan Haywood (7)
Binfield CE Primary School

OUR BOOK FESTIVAL

It was great, the crowds went wild,
You should have been there,
You should have been there,
Shall I buy this book?
Shall I buy that book?
You should have read this
You should have read that
You should have been there
You should have been there
The crowds went wild, it was great,
No time to stop and breathe
We've got to run to get to see her
What's her name?
What's her name?
Her name is Jacqueline Wilson
It was great, the crowds went wild
You should have been there
Yeah!

Nancy Reynolds (7)
Binfield CE Primary School

CHRISTMAS IS COMING

Christmas is coming!
Let the tinsel hang,
Let the drums bang,
Christmas is coming!
Have every present wrapped up
In sparkly red and green paper,
Christmas is coming!
With Santa coming down,
And go shopping in the town.
Christmas is coming!
Let's just have a little while,
To think who was born,
Christmas is coming!
Who was born?
Jesus was born,
Let a bright star shine,
To let us know
Why Christmas is here.
And . . . Christmas is here
today!

Katherine Mitchell (7)
Binfield CE Primary School

HOME SWEET HOME

My home is special to me
It has all my toys
It is warm and cosy
My home is special to me
It keeps me safe
All my family love me.

Lisa Clark (6)
Binfield CE Primary School

MY TEDDY BEAR

My teddy is special to me
She is warm and soft
I love my teddy
My teddy is grey
When my teddy is happy
I am happy
My teddy is special to me
I like it when my teddy cuddles me
I like it when my teddy sits on the
                                    window sill
My teddy is special to me.

Amelia Metcalfe (7)
Binfield CE Primary School

IT'S WASHDAY

Hot water in the sink
The washboard is in the sink
Scrub-a-dub-dub
Went the slippery soap.
In goes the washing
Scrub-a-dub-dub
We got our hands all slippery
And we got our hands as wet as could be.
And I put the washing in the mangle
And out on the line to dry.

Samantha Vickery (6)
Binfield CE Primary School

WORKING AT THE BINFIELD BRICKWORKS

I'm working at the Binfield brickworks
It's such hard work,
I'm mushing and crushing
the squishy wet clay
I'm working at the Binfield brickworks
It's such hard work,
I'm working and working
all day long.
I'm working at the Binfield brickworks
It's such hard work,
The foreman says,
Hey, you get on and you might get your shilling
I always think I'll never get 100 bricks done
to get a shilling.
The foreman is so mean
My hands are aching
I'm working at the Binfield brickworks
It's such hard work,
I'm putting the clay into moulds
My hands are wet and horrible,
I'm working at the Binfield brickworks
It's such hard work,
I go home, I can hardly walk
I am so exhausted
I could fall fast asleep
My hands are dry
And my skin is falling off
I'm working at the Binfield brickworks
It's such hard work.

James Parker (7)
Binfield CE Primary School

MAGIC!

Wizards and witches
Bubbling brew
Lizards' tails, newts' eyes
Frogs' legs too

Cauldrons, cooking pots
Wands and brooms
Spell books, pointed hats
Cobwebbed rooms

Talking pictures
Owls and cats
Green liquids
Moving mats

Worms and snakes
Eyeballs, tongues
Dragons' toenails
Leopards' lungs

All of this and much, much more
You will find beyond a door
In a land far, far away
I don't think you'll want to stay.

Elizabeth Mary Williams (9)
Brightwalton Primary School

BOOKS, BOOKS

I love books
I can stay in bed
Reading in my head
Dick King Smith
Roald Dahl
Ted Hughes
He gives us all the news
Also I love poems like:
'Tiger, Tiger, in the night' and
'On the Ding Dang Dong'
Now let's not make this poem too long
So if you're bored
Instead of getting in a nook
Why don't you read a book?

Becky Gills (10)
Brightwalton Primary School

MOTORBIKES

Kawasaki, Yamaha
Motorbikes galore,
Suzuki, BMW.
Come on give me more,
Ducati is the fastest bike,
Harley Davidson? Take a hike,
Honda Fireblades are pretty quick,
The Triumph 2 just makes me sick,
Husaberg and Husqvarna aren't very well-known
And Aprilla brings me to the end of my poem.

William Clarke (10)
Brightwalton Primary School

MY BEST FRIEND

My best friend keeps all types of pets
He brought them to school one day
Cockroaches in the kitchen
A hedgehog on the teacher's chair by mistake
Chameleons on the ceiling and
Terrapins in the sink
A bird bombing the test due for next week
A scorpion saw a
Tasty snack!

Stephen Kensett (10)
Brightwalton Primary School

THE HAUNTED HOUSE

The haunted house at the end of the road.
I try not to think about it.
It took my brother yesterday and I haven't seen him since.
Is he happy? Is he sad?
If he is sad, the house will be flooded!
I will be brave and go and see,
I turned the doorknob, what did I see?
My brother was safe and sound and screaming
'I'm free!'

Charlotte Yates (9)
Brightwalton Primary School

MOLE

There once was a mole
Digging in his hole
When a vole came and
Stole Mole's hole.

Mole was most upset
That Vole had stole his hole
So he ate his pet
Vole found out and was upset.

Meanwhile Mole decided to go for a dig,
When he was digging he found a pole.
Mole took the pole through his hole
And back to his home
Then he went
Through the hole that Vole had stole
And with his pole he poked Vole
Out of his hole and Mole was happy
That he had his hole that Vole had stole.

Hannah Simms (9)
Brightwalton Primary School

SNOW

It lies there
Still and soft,
Crisp and crunchy
Like icing on a cake,
Just waiting to be trodden on.
A blanket of ice over Earth.

Margaret Williams (11)
Brightwalton Primary School

RAIN OF DEATH

Sirens whirr, buildings alight
It's the Second World War, we are in a big fight.
I've joined the army, we're going strong,
And as we go to war, we sing our song.
I'm in the trenches with nerves of steel
But then I fall and pain I feel.
I can't find my legs, we've been hit by a shell,
And rotting flesh I can smell.
I crawl to my feet but fall over again.
I poke up my head, there's a mass of dead bodies.
I crawl and crawl to the enemy line,
They can't see me but I can see them.
I throw a grenade, that's the end of them.
I crawl to the trench, it's an alien world
       full of dead bodies and spent bullets.
New recruits coming to fight
I've got to hide, oh God, it's a plight.
I can see them, it's the end,
On my gun I have to depend.
I jump to sight with my gun ablaze
They're coming at me, they're all a haze.
Arrrgh! I can feel pain in my chest,
I can see light, it's the end of me,
       it's the end of my fight.
The war carried on and the English won
My folks mourn but they know I'm up there
Singing my song in the midnight air.

Alex Whiscombe (10)
Brightwalton Primary School

BIRDS

There are lots of different kinds of birds,
They are fascinating colours,
Blue, green, yellow, white, black, red and lots of others.
One of my favourite birds is the robin,
It's small, red, brown and gorgeous,
It flies with the wind,
There are lots of different kinds of birds,
Although they are all fascinating.

Galina Zoë Ananin (11)
Brightwalton Primary School

MY SINGING TOOTHBRUSH

Sing, sing, sing along
Sing along with me.
Brush, brush, brush my teeth all day
And be a friend to me.

Darren Roberts (10)
Coley Park Primary School

NATURE

Trees, leaves and one farm.
The sun setting near a barn.
Animals running through the woods
And a big stream making floods.

Billy Robinson (10)
Coley Park Primary School

FREDERICK PAR

Frederick Par
Was the greatest pop star,
He had a great big long car,
He didn't go far
In his great big car.
As he blew up the car,
He died in that car
In a country called America.

Antony Searle (11)
Coley Park Primary School

THE LADY

She walks, talks, lives and breathes.
Her hair, ratted and tatted like leaves.
She's unhappy, lonely, confident but brief.
She sits in the cafe waiting for her long lost love.
But still, no one comes to rescue her from above.

Jade Edwards (11)
Coley Park Primary School

MY FISH

My fish is slimy and slithery.
It curls and swirls.
It jumps and it thumps.
It swims fierce, and it swims gently.

Ben Holland (10)
Coley Park Primary School

CATS EVERYWHERE

Cat, Cat,
High upon the tree
Cat, Cat,
Walking on me.

Cat, Cat,
Walking on the air
Cat, Cat,
Falling through the air.

Cat, Cat,
Sliding on walls
Cat, Cat,
Slipping on tools.

Cat, Cat,
Purring to sleep,
Cat, Cat,
Falling to sleep.

Nicola Tiley (11)
Coley Park Primary School

TREE HOUSE

I have a big lovely tree house
It is the best of all.
No one knows I have a tree house,
Only me, my friends,
And other animals.
I only go to my tree house,
When I am upset.
I like my tree house.

Margaret Kanu (11)
Coley Park Primary School

CELEBRATIONS

C ome and join in all the fun.
E aster time, out comes the sun.
L ove is in the air, here's St Valentine,
E motional tears as you romantically dine.
B irthdays bring sadness and joy
R unning around with your gifts and toys
A ny time of the year will do,
T rees for Christmas, they matter too.
I roning isn't really fun.
O pening presents must be done
N ever, ever, is there not a time when
S easons and celebrations bring
                        love and rhyme.

Victoria Uwannah (10)
Coley Park Primary School

MY DAD HAS THE YEAR 2000 GEAR

My dad has the year 2000 gear
My dad has got the year 2000 computer
My dad has the year 2000 jokes
My dad has got the year 2000 books
My dad has the year 2000 movies
My dad has got the year 2000 clothes
My dad has the year 2000 shoes
My dad has got the year 2000 pets
My dad has the year 2000 food
My dad has the year 2000 technology
My dad has not got the year 2000 because
everyone has it.

Elizabeth Hobbs (9)
Francis Baily Primary School

NIGHT-TIME

Night-time is when I can see
Shadows in the hallway,
Shadows scaring me,
Shadows on the wall,
Shadows thin and shadows tall.

It's night-time, night-time.

Night-time is when I can hear,
The rumble of lorries passing far and near.
There's a mouse
Scurrying around our house.

It's night-time, night-time.

There's a cat crying at someone's door,
I've got the shivers and can't stand this anymore,
I try to get myself to sleep,
By counting lots of fluffy sheep.

It's night-time, night-time.

Oh! What is that face staring through at me?
It's just the moon that I can see,
That loud noise sounds like a lion roaring,
But thank goodness it's just my *dad* snoring.

It's night-time, night-time and now I'm asleep.

Chloe Whitehead (10)
Francis Baily Primary School

THE CRAZY HOUSE

The crazy house all white and blue
Standing with the bathroom loo,
On a great big, dazzling hill
The crazy house is standing still.

When people come to view the house
It turns itself into a mouse,
And when they've gone, the house comes back
All horrible and scary black.

Until the next day has arrived
The house will think it's not alive,
But when it finds that it can move
It loses all its upset mood.

It jumps and dances all around
And makes a massive thrilling sound,
Until it gets all tired out
It starts to remember a serious doubt.

That it's the only house in the world
Who can sing, dance and even twirl,
Sometimes it gets so upset
It won't dance until sunset.

When everything is dark and still
The house is sleeping on the hill,
Until the next day starts to come
The house will sleep sucking its thumb.

That's all I know about the house.

And now I'm going to feed my mouse,
But if you want to learn some more
You'll have to check to be sure.

Lorraine Bobb (10)
Francis Baily Primary School

CLOUDS

I lay on my back to look up at the sky
And dreamily watch the clouds drift by,
Spiralling, turning so fluffy and white,
On a hot summer's day, a wonderful sight.

There's a castle, with its giant tower
No wait a moment, perhaps it's a flower.
Now I can see a grizzly bear
And a fire-breathing dragon is over there.

Here comes another one, a fast-running dog
Hey, no it's not, it's a leaping frog!
So many forms the clouds can take
There's many more that they can make.

I could lie here all day, watching clouds come and go,
But now the sun is getting low,
The day's almost over, the darkness so near
And I'd better go home before night is here.

Nicky Long (10)
Francis Baily Primary School

THE MAN-EATING MONSTERS

Thud! Thud! Thud!
The man-eating monsters are here
Thud! Thud! Thud!
You'd better keep clear

Boom! Boom! Boom!
They're on their way
Boom! Boom! Boom!
They're coming today

Crunch! Crunch! Crunch!
He's picked someone out
Crunch! Crunch! Crunch!
Now he's getting quite stout

Snort! Snort! Snort!
The number of people is getting quite short
Snort! Snort! Snort!
If he carries on he'll go to court

Thud! Boom! Crunch! Snort!

Rhian Ellis (10)
Francis Baily Primary School

THE BOX OF MANY DREAMS

I will put in my box . . .

The cry of a baby on a winter's day,
The laughter of a girl singing on an autumn day.
I will put in my box . . .
The howl of the wolf which was never seen,
The birth of a baby cub.

My box is made of gold
sparkling like never seen,
with planets on the lid,
its hinges are made of the teeth of the last hound.

I would sail the Seven Seas,
swim with the biggest whale ever found.
I would make friends
With the last mammal ever known.

Joshua Davies (10)
Loddon Junior School

THE MAGIC BOX

I will put in the box . . .

A cold breeze on a hot neck on a summer's day
The glitter of the sun against a clear swimming pool
And the laugh from someone being tickled.

I will put in the box . . .

The warmth from a blazing fire
The power of a dozen elephants
The love from all my family.

I will put in the box . . .

The sigh as an everlasting life comes to a halt
And the cry of a newborn baby.
My box is covered with the skin of the ripest peach
And crystal stones.

Jamie Girdler (10)
Loddon Junior School

THE MAGIC BOX

I will put in the box . . .

The sound of a shoe snapping dry twigs,
The crunch of the snow as gloves pick it up,
The cry of a spider as it takes its last breath,
The twinkle of the stars on a cool summer's night.

I will put in the box . . .

The frustration you feel when you can't spell a word,
The breath of a cat when it's just run a mile,
The groan of a cow as she lies down to die,
And the first moo of a newly born calf.

My box is fashioned delicately,
The sides are made from plaited daisies,
The lid is made from all the colours of the rainbow,
The base is a floor of marigolds and tulips,
And the hinges are made from prickles and thorns.

In my box I will build a raft,
And sail to where the dolphins play,
They'll be my friends forever,
And protect me and carry me away.

Anna Elliott (11)
Loddon Junior School

MY MAGIC BOX

I will put in my box . . .

The smell of flowers when they first bloom in spring,
The shine of the sun on the first day of summer,
The crunch of leaves as they crumble under your foot on an
autumn day,
The flow of the falling snow on a cold winter's morning.

I will put in my box . . .

The sound of the sea as it laps on the sand,
The last jump of a horse,
And the first whinny of a foal,
The glimmer of the moon in the starry night sky.

My box is made of the finest jewels in the world,
The lid is covered in the smoothest silk,
And the hinges made from an elephant's toenails.

In my box I shall sail around the world,
And land on the sun.

Gemma Donnelly (11)
Loddon Junior School

MY MAGIC BOX

I will put in my box . . .

The sound of the leaves as they sway in the wind,
A dog giving its last bark,
A kitten giving its first miaow,
And a shell giving out the sound of the sea.

I will put in my box . . .

The crunch of the snow as you take a step,
The happiness you feel when you get something new,
The squeak of a mouse as it runs to its hole,
And the smell of an ancient book as you open it up.

My box is fashioned by silver and gold,
And the sparkle of stars surround it,
The hinges are made of stiff hard silk,
And the lid is a field of brass.

In my box I will swim with dolphins and whales,
I'll build my own ship made from coconut trees,
And I'll sail the wild and wavy seas.

Emma Paintin (11)
Loddon Junior School

THE MAGIC BOX

I will put in the box . . .

A gentle breeze
The most beautiful flowers
The most silky clouds
A star so beautiful that it will become part of your life
The mother's broken heart when she first sees her fresh newborn
baby's face.

The box is fashioned by the silky golden lid and the handle made out of lead crystal, the box itself is made by the most beautiful rainbow-coloured seashells.

I would like to live in the environment of the box and get wishes from it.

Robert Callard (11)
Loddon Junior School

THE MAGIC BOX

I will put in my box . . .

The scent of a bunch of red roses on a breezy day,
The sound of a newborn baby crying,
A hand touching the silky coat of a small puppy,
And the laughter of young children laughing at a clown.

I will put in my box . . .

The sound of a big celebration,
The last cry of a cat's miaow,
The first sight of its tabby kitten,
A delicate hand touching a shining star in the sky.

My box is fashioned by some armour from a fighting knight,
Some gold and silver from an ancient mine,
A shooting star from the twinkling sky,
And some wild flowers to cover the magical magic.

In my box I will see the whole world,
Buy lots of animals to look after,
I will swim with dolphins in the deep blue sea,
And travel to the galaxy and back.

Emily Jones (11)
Loddon Junior School

THE MAGIC BOX

I will put in the box . . .

The smash of a conker as it falls to the ground,
And the crunch of the autumn leaves as people walk over them.

I will put in the box . . .

The light from a shooting star as it sails over the midnight sky,
And the glare of the burning sun when it's shining onto us.

My box is fashioned with gold, silver and bronze,
With pictures of the sun, moon and all the planets carved into it.

In the box everyone will rise into the sky with the fireworks and
explode into a million colours,
Then come sailing down and make everyone's dreams come true.

Helen Lusby (11)
Loddon Junior School

THE MAGIC BOX

I will put in my box . . .
A lovely, silky, slithering snake
on a warm desert,
and the sound of wild horses.

My box is fashioned with sparkles of the sun on the ocean
and a lovely cloud like snow from the sky like silk.

My box will be sailed in the silky ocean
where the magic will spread over the poor countries
to all the suffering, weak, cuddly children.

Kerri-Lee Rumbold (11)
Loddon Junior School

MY MAGIC BOX

I will put in my box . . .

The scent of a flower on a warm spring morn,
The glint of the stars, high in the sky,
And the sound of a foot, crunching on shells.

I will put in my box . . .

The very first drop of falling rain,
The heat of the glistening sun,
The sound of the ants, as they hurry about,
And the silence of a sleeping child.

My box is fashioned with silver and gold,
And the purest wood from a walnut tree,
Its inside is covered by the sound of thousands of macaws,
Talking their funny talk to me.

In my box I will see the world,
As I travel around with the birds,
I can do what I want,
See whatever I wish,
When I am in my box.

Abigail Hope (11)
Loddon Junior School

THE MAGIC BOX

I will put into the box,
The sound of a kitten's first miaow,
The swish of the first goal,
And the first wind in the world.

I will put into the box,
The last howl of a wolf,
The last laugh of an only grandad,
And the first smile of a baby.

My box is fashioned
Of bright blue and red gemstones,
And the finest silk,
With one hundred jokes scattered around.

I will waterski in my box,
On the calmest lake,
And come in on a sandy shore.

Kevin Cahill (11)
Loddon Junior School

THE LITTLE WHITE RABBIT

The little white rabbit is so sweet,
He has enormous big feet,
And you never know what he will meet.

He has big, floppy ears,
And then he peers
To look at the galloping deers.

Michaela Tegg (9)
Park Lane Primary School

TIGER

Sharp
claws
Big
paws
Running
tiger
Frightened
man
Warriors
fighting
All
exciting
Tiger
killed
All
silent.

Perry Tomlin (9)
St Anthony's RC Primary School, Slough

THE NIGHTMARE

The wind blows beneath your toes,
It may be scary;
So be wary,
The dark and the wind are my foes.

The light goes click (silence),
The wind whistles
Through the thistles,
The clock goes tick, tock, tick.

Shane Martin Cole (10)
St Anthony's RC Primary School, Slough

PEANUT BUTTER

I love peanut butter,
I'll have it with jam,
I'll have it with mustard,
I'll have it with ham.

I love it for my tummy,
I smooth it like paste,
I mix it with honey,
It gives it a sweet taste.

My mum and dad love vindaloo,
My dog drinks out of the loo,
My sister likes tomato sauce,
My brother doesn't eat any course.

But my favourite's got to be,
Peanut butter and honey.

Rhys Haslam (9)
St Anthony's RC Primary School, Slough

THERE'S AN AWFUL LOT OF WEIRDOES IN MY NEIGHBOURHOOD

There's a man in a window staring at me,
There's a lady dressed up as a bumblebee.
There's witches flying around my house,
The road's blocked up by a great big mouse.

There's a ghost outside with a cannonball,
There's a little old lady building a wall.
There's Donald Duck in the bath,
Then there's me who's just plain daft.

Billy Coulson (10)
St Anthony's RC Primary School, Slough

GETTING UP

As I hear the birds in the skies,
That's the moment I open my eyes,
I look around,
I can only hear one sound.

My alarm wakes me up in a dip,
I remember I have to fix my zip,
Then I look at the time,
I had to meet Nanny at nine.

I then put my clothes on,
Then I was out of the door, gone,
There I was all alone,
Strangely I picked up the phone.

I put down the phone like before
Ding dong, I had to open the door,
At the door stood my own mum,
I hoped she had something for my tum.

'Mum, Mum, look at the time,
I thought we were going to meet Nanny at nine?'
'Oh! Oh! Yes! Yes!'
'Calm down or you'll get in a mess!'

Shanice Akinyombo (9)
St Anthony's RC Primary School, Slough

MY WORM

I have a little, friendly worm
His name is Billy-Joe
I take him to school and Cubs and things
In fact, everywhere I go!

My worm is brown and wriggly
And smooth, shiny and fat
He makes me feel all giggly
When I hide him under my hat.

Billy-Joe is my best mate
He makes me feel so good
My friends say they'd like to keep a worm
If only they could.

One day when walking down the street
A large bird came flying close by
He took a look at Billy-Joe
And soon the end was nigh
He plucked him out of my top pocket
And swallowed him up.

Adam Hinds (10)
St Anthony's RC Primary School, Slough

SOCCER

Luke Hill is my name,
Soccer is my game.
Every day I kick a ball,
To the cheers of one and all.
Nine is the one,
And I run like a gun.

Ginola is the best,
But we put him to the test,
Soccer is a game of two halves,
And sometimes in the game we have some laughs.
The ref is the person in charge,
And sometimes we can be very hard.

Luke Hill (10)
St Anthony's RC Primary School, Slough

GRUNTY

Grunty's my pig,
He's enormously big.
He's bored all day,
And never wants to play.
When I'm in school,
At home he acts the fool.
He never stops eating,
But I've never given him a beating.
When I'm not looking, he devours my lunch,
I really feel like giving him a punch.
The most embarrassing thing,
Was when he tried to sing.
He grunted a note,
And I hid under my coat.
Everyone shut their ears,
By now I was in tears.
But although his actions are unknown,
He's not as idle as a bone.
He's fluffy and cuddly,
And he's my pet, Grunty.

Duane Fernandes (10)
St Anthony's RC Primary School, Slough

WAR

War is as black as the sky at night,
It is not like the sun shining bright.
War smells like people burning,
It's like your freedom turning.
War tastes like black ashes,
All smoky like plane crashes.
War sounds like bodies exploding,
A truck full of bodies loading.
War feels like the dead in fields,
But war does not involve gun shields.
War lives in fields of death,
It's a crime of body theft.
Then comes the good part,
Freedom at last,
War is behind us,
It's in the past.

Joseph Hullait (10)
St Anthony's RC Primary School, Slough

UP THE CHIMNEY

My name is Peter,
I'm off to work again
Up the chimney,
Up so high
With all my might.
Grazed and cut,
Bumped and bruised,
Up I go so high.
I sniff and I sneeze
In the dark chimney.

Jack Carroll (10)
St Anthony's RC Primary School, Slough

ANOTHER LONG DAY

I am a chimney sweep,
I don't like it but it earns my keep.
Up the chimneys I climb,
All the soot I find.
I get cuts on my knees and elbows,
Oh no, on the salt goes.
It stings so much I just can't bear it,
Silly master, Mr McClarit.

I do not get paid much for my time,
All the chimneys I have to climb.
All of this dust doesn't do much for my chest,
But there's so much to do, there's no time for a rest.
Lower and lower I climb down,
I stop, think of my life and just frown.
I wish I could leave, I wish I could go,
How I'll get out of here, I just don't know.

I'll tell you a tale of my friend, Ross,
Who worked for a man they called Boss,
Ross climbed the chimney and got lost.
Boss cried at the boy to come down,
But Ross was there stuck fast and sound.
The lady cried with such a frown,
'What can be done if he can't be found?'
Boss scratched his head and looked around,
'I'll buy lots more for just a pound.'

Kelly Tushingham (10)
St Anthony's RC Primary School, Slough

THE PROMISE

'Why do you leave us to fight and travel in the army,
   for you know your mother is ill?'
'It is my duty to fight for our country,
   you know very well it is!'
'But it is so dangerous out there on the battlefield.'
   'Do not worry, a bullet will not pierce my flesh.
Once the war is over; I promise I will come home!'
   But the war was longer, much longer than I thought.
After each battle another one had to be fought.
   And so it happened, I was shot,
About noon I'd say.
   As the lead bullet ripped open my skin,
I gave out a cry.
   'Twas like poison pumping through my body.
As I lay on the battlefield, so dense with death,
   I remembered my promise and said quietly;
'I shall survive, go home to mother and father, as I promised them so.'
   After the war was over, I went home.
On the path I saw some used bullets and bravely walked up to the door.

Christopher Rakowski (10)
St Anthony's RC Primary School, Slough

GETTING UP!

I was getting up in the morning,
But I was still yawning,
I was trying to get out of bed,
But I bashed my head.

I put my slippers and things on,
And then I was downstairs, gone.
My sister was very loud, screaming,
She made sure I didn't start dreaming.

I went in the bathroom to have a wash,
And the water went slosh, slosh, slosh.
Then I changed clothes for school,
And I felt really cool.

Stephen Wallace (10)
St Anthony's RC Primary School, Slough

A SWEEP'S LIFE

It's 6am, the sky is grey,
Lots of chimneys to sweep today.

Cuts and bruises on my legs and chest,
From climbing up the chimney breast.

The rich people in their houses do not see,
What life is like for a sweep like me.

Up at dawn for very little pay,
Sometimes I want to run away.

The master's mean, he treats me wrong,
Even though I work all day long.

He lights a fire if I'm not quick,
The smell of the smoke makes me sick.

When I'm too big to be a sweep,
I'll have to earn my own keep.

Until then, up the chimney I will crawl,
Thankful that I have work at all.

Robert Thomas Mehta (11)
St Anthony's RC Primary School, Slough

ANOTHER LONG DAY

My day starts at 3 o'clock,
Cut and grazed from the day before,
I shall not finish 'til 12 o'clock,
After cleaning chimneys once more.

My master rubs in salt,
To harden the skin,
And pricks our feet
With a pin.

There's just one thing
That would be so dear,
It's to have a bath
More than once a year.

Sammy-Jo Higgins (11)
St Anthony's RC Primary School, Slough

A BEAUTIFUL SUMMER'S DAY

I woke up this morning,
Feeling tired and yawning.
I started getting dressed,
And tried to look my best.
I ate my toast, I fed my cat,
Put on my shoes and summer hat.
I then went out in the garden to play,
To enjoy a beautiful summer's day.
The sky was blue, the grass was green,
It was the loveliest day I'd ever seen.

Kirsty Wilks (11)
St Anthony's RC Primary School, Slough

ANOTHER LONG DAY

It's 6am, the sky is grey,
I know I'm going to have a terrible day.

My master's very, very mean,
His name doesn't suit him, it's Mr Green.

He gives me a fright,
I can't do anything right.

Climbing up the chimney high,
There's no sight of the sky.

I hope I'm very near the top,
I also hope I'll not drop.

Now I'm glad the work can halt,
But now of course there comes the salt.

For rubbing into cuts and scrapes,
That's the stuff I really hate.

At last the time for fun and games,
No more shouts and beats and blames.

Watching horses trotting by,
Tossing heads up to the sky.

Then comes the time for supper and bed,
Time to rest my weary head.

Boys all round try to sleep,
Praying that they'll slumber deep.

Michael Hargadon (11)
St Anthony's RC Primary School, Slough

UP THE CHIMNEY

I wake up at dawn,
And continue to yawn,
As I struggle to get out of bed.
The sky is grey,
I'll have another terrible day,
And I can't get the sleep out of my head.

Master's name is Cox,
He's a vicious fox,
I'm his slave and he doesn't care.
Up the chimney I go,
Not allowed to go slow,
And I breathe in the filthy air.

Once my brush got stuck,
Amongst all that muck,
So I had to go and get it.
Cox said I was slow,
And stuck a pin up my toe,
And shouted, 'Hurry up or you'll regret it.'

Chimneys are poky,
They're black and they're smoky,
Why do I work in this terrible place?
I sweat and choke,
From the terrible smoke,
And I'm covered with bruises from my toes to my face.

My body is tired,
My fingers are sore,
And yet I've another ten chimneys more.
I lay down my head,
On my blackened bed,
Unable to do another chore.

Adam Pierozynski (10)
St Anthony's RC Primary School, Slough

PLEASE MISS GREEN

Please Miss Green
This girl Nicky Drew
Just snapped my pencil
What shall I do?

Go and sit on the loo dear
Go and sit in the hall
Go and sit on the roof my lamb
But don't play with the ball.

Please Miss Green
This girl Nicky Drew
She's just pinched my ear
What shall I do?

Go and sit in the playground
Sit on another table
Go and sit in the bath
Or go and make a label.

Sarah Viney (9)
St Nicolas Junior School, Newbury

PLEASE MR TWIG

Please Mr Twig
This body Dexter Lloyd
He keeps pulling my hair Sir
What shall I do?

Go and sit outside my dear
Or sit on the roof and rest
Go do what you like dear
Do what you think's best.

Rebecca Barnes (9)
St Nicolas Junior School, Newbury

PLEASE MISS MARGON

Please Miss Margon
This boy Billy Drew
Keeps taking my pencil
What shall I do?

Go and sit on the roof dear
Go and sit on the clock
Take yourself into the basement my lamb
And undo the lock!

Please Miss Margon
This boy Billy Drew
Is hurting me Miss
What shall I do?

Go and sing a hymn,
Go and sit in the corner,
Go and sit on the swing
Or move to another table!

Please Miss Margon
This boy Billy Drew
Keeps taking my ruler Miss,
What shall I do?

Joanne Smith (8)
St Nicolas Junior School, Newbury

A SHELL

A crusty edge just like it's come out of an oven,
Some spiky points just to keep it up on its feet,
A crispy burnt edge like it's just come back from the beach,
It's like it's been on an exciting adventure.

Alexander McGregor (9)
St Nicolas Junior School, Newbury

GHOSTLY SOUNDS

Our house is haunted, ghosts clicking, clacking
The landing's shivering and the dogs are howling.

Clicking, clacking on our landing,
My lampshade's glittering on the ceiling.

Our house is haunted, ghosts screaming,
Yelling, screaming, yelling, howling.

Clicking, clacking on our landing,
My lampshade's glittering on the ceiling.

Our house is haunted, ghosts banging,
Hitting, screaming, yelling.

Becky Tait (8)
St Nicolas Junior School, Newbury

WHISTLE WOO

Whistle woo, whistle woo
The mouth of the owl goes tu-whit tu-whoo
Screeching past as it flies through the air
And lands on the roof so very bare.

Whistle woo, what can you do
When it's so scary around you?
Why won't you say whistle woo all day?

Whistle woo, whistle woo
The mouth of the owl goes tu-whit tu-whoo
Screeching past at flies through the air
And lands on the roof so very bare.

Kimberley Coffman (9)
St Nicolas Junior School, Newbury

PLEASE MR BRAIDE

Please Mr Braide
This boy Arthur Brew
Keeps ripping up my work Sir
What shall I do?

Go and sit in a mole hole
Go and sit in the sink
Take a rocket up to space dear
Do what ever you think?

Please Mr Braide
This boy Arthur Brew
Keeps kicking my leg Sir
What shall I do?

Go and break your leg bone
Put it up your vest
Go and sit on the roof my lamb
Do what you think's best!

Please Mr Braide
This boy Arthur Brew
Keeps using my rubber Sir
What shall I do?

Keep it in your hand dear
Tie it on a bee
Hide it in your desk my lamb
But don't ask me!

Kelly Dobie (8)
St Nicolas Junior School, Newbury

FREDDY THE MOUSE

The sun is shining down
The moon has gone away
I am out of bed early
On this bright summer day.

I like the hot, smiling sun
So I am going out to play
Oh, I have to feed my horse
With fresh lovely hay.

It's raining, oh I can't play
So I play in the house
I am bored playing inside
What is that on the floor . . .
A mouse.

I call my mousey Freddy
Freddy's gone into his hole
He is not going to come out
But I saw him on a pole.

I showed Mummy Freddy
Oops Mummy's on the floor
Daddy came home
He is standing at the door.

Daddy said he will get Mummy up
So I go to bed
I went and climbed into bed
But I hit my head.

Mummy felt better
After her little fright
So she came upstairs to kiss me and
Said 'Sleep tight.'

Sarah Morgan (9)
St Nicolas Junior School, Newbury

MEADOW

Children playing in the grass,
Ladies wandering amongst the flowers,
Grass shimmering in the evening sun,
The tree swings from side to side,
The pond shines brightly as day breaks,
The wind blowing the tree branches.

Natasha Jones (9)
St Nicolas Junior School, Newbury

A ROBOT'S JOB

Bang, wham, smashing
Crash, smash, hitting,
That is a robot's job.

Clattering, clittering,
Kicking and jumping,
That is a robot's job.

Helping and carrying,
Driving and lifting,
That is a robot's job.

Fitting, taking,
Expanding, shrinking,
That is a robot's job.

Working, running,
What is coming?
Now I'm exploding!

Daniel Groszek (8)
St Nicolas Junior School, Newbury

EXCUSES! EXCUSES!

My pencil walked out the door Miss
My rubber flew away
My pencil case told me to go home Miss
Every single day

My knee has gone all wobbly Miss
My pencil has gone all blunt
My ruler snapped in half Miss
My book's all back to front

My reading book's jumped out the window Miss
My head banged on the floor
My leg stuck to the chair Miss
And everybody swore

My friend threw an apple Miss
My paper broke in half
My poem is all stupid
Oh, what a laugh.

Matthew Gregory (8)
St Nicolas Junior School, Newbury

CRASH, SMASH, BANG IN THE KITCHEN

Crashing dishes,
Smashing plates,
These are the sounds the kitchen makes.

Sizzling pans,
Banging sieves,
These are the sounds the kitchen gives.

Roaring ovens,
Turning microwaves,
These are the sounds the kitchen says.

Swishing taps,
Water whooshing,
These are the sounds the kitchen sings.

Smoke alarm screeching,
Clock ticking,
These are the sounds the kitchen makes.

James Hunter (8)
St Nicolas Junior School, Newbury

NIGHT

The night is as dark as coal,
The moon is creeping along the sky shining brightly through the clouds,
The stars are twinkling amazingly.

Cold and shivering, people run by,
Looking down on the houses, looking down on the roofs,
Creeping round with my candle, it blew out,
The shadows dance.

Now the house is gloomy, I can't see anything,
As the stars sprinkle light through the window,
I see a flashing, flickering light,
I run outside to see, it's a cat blinking.

There I stand in the darkness,
The air scratching my face as it goes by,
The moon staring down on me,
The shops all closed and quiet.

I run along a bit further, and what do I see?
A white, floating blanket of cloud floating down the street,
A tunnel of wool, I blink, I snuggle, I sleep.

Aimee Mitchard
St Nicolas Junior School, Newbury

MOANS AND GROANS

The teachers all bathe in the bathroom,
The teachers all dress up,
The teachers all pray for hometime,
They get drunk on 7up!

We can't go out when we want to,
We want to have some tuck,
We have to go out when it's raining,
And we all get covered in muck.

We have to earn our team points,
We have to work our best,
We have to listen to teachers,
We never get any rest.

The teachers report to our parents,
Whether we're good or bad,
The teachers read us extracts,
The teachers get so mad!

Lucy Wade (9)
St Nicolas Junior School, Newbury

UNTITLED

A treasure chest is in the deepness of the cave
Full of treasure, but what's that sooty thing buried in it

It's a rock, a magical rock, make your wish and it will come true
Say your wish then rub the rock, then your wish it will come true

The beautiful rock was forgotten, but now it's found
Now the rock is shining, gleaming in your hand

The rock looks like a dusty book hidden for years
The dusty shape is found now

The rock is no more a rock, but a lump of shining gold
Now you've found the forgotten rock, all your wishes will come true

The golden rock is now yours, yours forever, forever and ever
The blazing, glistening twinkle of the rock will be yours as long
                                                    as you live.

Anna Tomlinson (9)
St Nicolas Junior School, Newbury

THE TREE TRUNK

In our school we have a tree trunk,
Today it is in our classroom.
The tree trunk is very spectacular,
It looks like dinosaurs.
By the way it is shaped,
It looks like they are turned to stone.
The dinosaurs stare at you,
I feel terrible, terrified.
It's jagged and knobbly,
It gives me the creeps,
As I go by.
It is maze after maze of gloom,
If I went in I would get lost in a second,
Like someone leaping out.

Rachel Cleal (9)
St Nicolas Junior School, Newbury

THE WHALE

The whale is as big as a boat.
The song it makes sounds sad and distraught.
The blue mammal sprays water as it dives for prey.
As he plunges for delicate plankton.
The gentle creature doesn't notice the boats,
Trying to capture the whale for the new attraction.
How blind we are not to see this animal is a free one.
That mankind is destroying nature in its natural habitat.

This land isn't our land.
It isn't their land. It is everybody's.

Daniel Beach (9)
St Nicolas Junior School, Newbury

MISTY MOON

The humungous eyes of the ocean,
That stare at you at night,
The frosty moon floats over your head,
Hours until it's bright.

Then suddenly comes the face of brightness,
It blazes down on you,
It glows more happier than the light,
Of the misty moon.

The temptation of your body is telling you to go,
To go and visit the misty moon,
All night it's there to glow.

Then it comes before your eyes,
The frosty moon to glow,
It's now your chance to visit it,
And return in the dawn.

It's now time to come back home,
It's becoming dawn,
The moon has died,
But will come back soon,
To dazzle upon the lawn.

Jane Baker (9)
St Nicolas Junior School, Newbury

SUNSET

The sun is a red and orange fire pan. It is dead hot.
The sun is spectacular,
And if you put your thumb on it you will smudge the beautiful sun.
The sun is like a boiling hot fireball. The sun is breaking the clouds
                                                                    apart.

It's making the clouds die.
The sun is a giant pizza boiling to death.
The sun looks absolutely gorgeous,
It's like an orange spying through the clouds.
It is like a melon pinned to the deep see-through sky.
The sun is like a lightning arrow hitting the sun and bouncing on
                                                                the sun,
And deflecting off the sun and bouncing off different countries and
                                                                places.

The sun is a boiling hot spiral, waiting to die.

Paul Marshall (9)
St Nicolas Junior School, Newbury

GREEN IS . . .

Lovely green crunchy grass,
The water crashing against the rocks,
The green leaves swaying in the air,
A frog jumping like a rabbit,
A slithering slimy lizard,
The hopping green grasshopper,
A sneaky scaly snake,
Green apples have a lovely taste.

Adam Ostler (9)
St Peter's Middle School, Old Windsor

WHAT IS GOLD?

What is gold?
Is it wheat shining in the field,
Ready for harvest.
A field-mouse scurrying about collecting
Wheat for its nest.
The sun burning like fire in the sky,
Or the bars of gold robbers want
To get their hands on?
Is it gold hair shining in the sun,
A gateway to another world,
Or daffodils swaying gently in the
Mild breeze.
Is it sunflowers, big, bright and
Colourful.
Teddy bears that small children
Cuddle gleefully at night.
Or is it the World Cup shimmering
In the sunlight on its proud shelf.
What is gold?
Can you work it out?

Hannah Christie (9)
St Peter's Middle School, Old Windsor

BLUE

Slipping, dripping sky floating like cold ice.
Running, splashing dolphin swimming towards the bright moon.
Splashing clear Stuart dripping bold ink on my book.
Dangerous cold bluebells like dithering icicles in my veins.
Staring icy eyes, gazing over the shivering sea.

James Mooney (9)
St Peter's Middle School, Old Windsor

BLUE

Cold, dripping water from the sky is floating in the glitter
Of forget-me-knots.
Clear and bold water is running happily like the ink,
In my biro.
The light splashing colour of a bluebell, shimmering on the
Glistening waters edge.
The glitter in the eyes of the glistening bright moon.
Bold, flowing dolphins, skipping and running through
The ocean.

Alastair Sharpe (9)
St Peter's Middle School, Old Windsor

BLUE

Cold, clear sky shining towards a glittery Stuart.
Bubbling, splashing moon floating
Towards a shivering bluebell.
Glittering, shining pen swaying with
Dangerous ink.
Bright bubbling eyes slipping into
Ice water.
Swirling, flowing ink, dripping frosty
Icicles on to my homework diary.

Rebecca Taylor (9)
St Peter's Middle School, Old Windsor

GREEN

Green, green, green, how I like green.
Green is the soft mushy grass.
Green is jumping fat swamp frogs,
Green is my colour.

Killer eating mantas,
Quick, vicious alligators,
Slimy monster, Godzilla.

Green may mean to you,
A hot pea stew.
But I like it as a jungle
With beautiful green trees.

Not like ice, it's not even as nice.
So white I do not like,
Or red, or yellow, or blue,
But green is my colour,
For ever and ever,
And that is my colour to stay.

Andy Owens (9)
St Peter's Middle School, Old Windsor

BLUE

Happy, swaying sky is as bold as starlight,
Flowing fish are shivering in happy ink.
Splashing, flowing water is slipping out of a
Dangerous pen.
Gold glittering ink is dripping from an icy biro.
Clear shining sea is floating towards light water.

Ben Thorpe (9)
St Peter's Middle School, Old Windsor

GREEN

The lush green grass sways in the wind.
The snake slithers through it.
The leaves whisper in the trees.
A fresh apple rushes to the ground.
A grasshopper jumps into the air,
As a frog dives into the pond,
Disturbing the weeds.
The squawk of the parrot distracts the woodpecker.
The slimy green snail-trail leads to the pond.
A frog starts to chase a dragonfly,
A dragonfly lands on a lily pad.

Tony Barker (9)
St Peter's Middle School, Old Windsor

GREEN

Green is the trees swaying in the gentle breeze,
The soft wind blowing through the green grass,
Green is the scrummy smelling lettuce,
Fresh in the fridge.
Green is a slithery, slimy frog,
Hopping everywhere.
Green is a slippery lizard,
Crawling into its hole.
Green is an luminous green grasshopper,
Pouncing out of the long, tall grass.
Green is my favourite colour.

Liam Tomkins (9)
St Peter's Middle School, Old Windsor

GREEN IS THE COLOUR OF

Trees swaying in the cold breezes,
The grass that grows higher and higher to the sky,
The rough sea that fiercely crashes against the weathered rocks,
The beautiful black eyelashes blinking over the gorgeous
green eyes,
A slimy green frog leaping everywhere.

A happy child who has just won a Tudor merit mark,
A green grasshopper bouncing everywhere,
Fresh leaves floating slowly to the ground,
An apple crunching sickly in a hungry mouth,
A crocodile snapping at a stranded man in the jungle.

Christopher Black (9)
St Peter's Middle School, Old Windsor

BLUE

Blue is cold, icy, wet, and freezing.
Blue reminds me of the sea,
Waves, sky, snowflakes,
Rivers and lakes.
Blue is a cold Christmasy colour,
Blue reminds me of crystal
Raindrops falling from the sky.
An ink colour for a blue pen.
Blue can be a diamond!
A lovely diamond!

Lucy Bristow (9)
St Peter's Middle School, Old Windsor

GREEN IS . . .

Green is the crashing water weaving through the waves,
The football pitch being mown in straight lines.

Green is the gentle leaves falling from some trees,
The hopping frog leaping everywhere,
And Tudor House winning the merit mark chart.

Green is the bushes swaying in the wind,
And the sound of a felt-tip brushing against the paper,
And the slimy seaweed slipping through your hand,
And the fresh squidgy peas jumping everywhere.

Rachel Simpson (9)
St Peter's Middle School, Old Windsor

YELLOW

Yellow is the colour of the sun,
Shining brightly in the sky.
Yellow is the colour of the sand
As it sparkles in the light,
When people run over it,
And daffodils swaying in the gentle wind,
And a ripe banana lying in a fruit bowl.
A fierce fire, glowing,
As it shines in the dark.

Stephanie Waters (9)
St Peter's Middle School, Old Windsor

GREEN

Green is the colour of the newly mown grass.
Green is the colour of the leaves upon the trees.
Green is the colour of the frog in the pond.
Green is the colour of the grasshopper leaping to and fro.

Green is the rough sea throwing boats around.
Green is glowing cat's eyes twinkling on the water.
Green is the glaring alligator in the soup-green water.
Green is the gigantic crocodile stranded on the rock.
Green is my colour forever and ever.

Nicky Woodward (9)
St Peter's Middle School, Old Windsor

PINK

Pink is beautiful and bright,
Pink flowers are such a delight,
When I get embarrassed my face goes pink.
Pink is the colour of my favourite bubblegum drink.
Pigs are big, pink and fat.
The Pink Panther was known as the groovy cat.
Pink bubbles in my bath makes my baby brother laugh.
Pink pencils make my pictures look pretty.
I colour my hair pink for discos.
Pink is my favourite colour.

Isabel Somerville Baddeley (9)
St Peter's Middle School, Old Windsor

WHEN I THINK OF GREEN I THINK OF . . .

The wind moving the trees slowly,
green small peas and some squeezed ones.
Land is a shape that will be there forever.
The lovely eyelashes close over the
beautiful green eyes.
Seaweed long as the water moves
it up on the shore.
The long grass moves quickly in the wind.
In a pond some slimy, slippery frogs move about.
The bushes stand up like
soldiers in the wind.

Amy-Lee Paradise (9)
St Peter's Middle School, Old Windsor

I LOVE RED

The bloodshot eyes after tears,
Little children's nightmares full of their fears.
The St Peter's school jumpers that keep us warm,
The beautiful red sunset that fills the sky,
The blood that keeps us alive, feet to eyes.
Our heart to let us live.
The colour of heat in the warmth of the summer,
Oh, I really do love red wherever it may be,
The bads and goods, the don'ts and shoulds,
That all help me.

Adam Smiter (10)
St Peter's Middle School, Old Windsor

What Is Red?

Red is the blood rushing
And gushing through our body,
Pleasing to the eye is the
Red tulip glowing in the sun.
The glorious red petals
Of a rose holding its head up high,
Summer fruits, red strawberries,
Hidden in thick cream
Tiny red cherries tempting to eat.
Crunching delicious red apples
Catch your eye in the fruit shop.
Winter arrives, showing red in a different light.
Sitting inside, in front of
The open fire, which too has
Sparks of red.
I watch robin red-breast,
Sitting proudly on the garden wall.
Time for school!
And I wrap myself up in
My warm school jumper,
All comfy and red.
School's over, what's on telly?
Liverpool! What a brilliant sight,
Owen comes out in red!

Neha Sharma (9)
St Peter's Middle School, Old Windsor

YELLOW IS . . .

Yellow is my favourite colour,
Like the lovely sun setting above the sea.
Yellow is like the ripe banana
In the big bowl,
Yellow is the beautiful sunflower
Blowing in the gentle breeze.

Hearing the burning fire
From the hall, makes me think
Of yellow.
I think of yellow,
When I see a wild lion in the colourful jungle.
And buttercups in the enormous garden
In my favourite story.

Because I love sweetcorn it
Reminds me of yellow.
Now I will always think of yellow,
All the time.
Yellow is my favourite colour.

Sunita Patel (9)
St Peter's Middle School, Old Windsor

BLUE IS . . .

The beautiful sunlight glimmering on the sea water,
The bluebells, swaying in the cool breeze.
A shark gliding through the water.
The blue school diary bulging with writing.
The cloudy, colourful sky,
The blue Dedworth jumper worn by joyful children.
My favourite colour is blue.

Callum Hall (9)
St Peter's Middle School, Old Windsor

MY LIFE IS FULL OF BLUE

My life is full of blue,
I gaze into the deep cloud,
Sorrow-filled sky
And realise that in my soul,
I am blue.
I look in the mirror,
And tear-stained, mournful blue eyes
Stare back at me.
At school I stare at my
Blue ink-filled pen, thinking,
There is blue everywhere!
Books in the library, their pages
Ruffling mysteriously.
The fierce sea, crashing
Against the rocks.
And lastly, the peaceful bluebell.
My life is full of blue.

Helen May-Bowles (10)
St Peter's Middle School, Old Windsor

GREEN

Green is. . .
The gentle breeze blowing the ancient trees,
And the great wind swaying the long, green grass.
Out of the grass leaps the mighty grasshopper,
While the lazy fat frog basks on a giant lily pad.
Green is juicy apples falling from the large trees above,
Green is the colour of nature.

Ben Allen (9)
St Peter's Middle School, Old Windsor

BLUE

When I think of blue, I think of
The sky, blue, blank, huge, dark,
And soothing.

When I think of blue, I think of
Rough sea, like a horse cantering.

When I think of blue, I think of
Colourful clothes like a box of paints.

When I think of blue, I think of
Splashing and sploshing,
And jumping in puddles.

When I think of blue, I think of
A swaying bluebell in the breeze,
Like a bell ringing.

When I think of blue, I think of
A long river like a snake moving,
Smoothly.

When I think of blue, I think of
A gigantic whale like a giant swimming
In the water.

When I think of blue, I think of
A dolphin jumping and joking,
Like a monkey in the jungle.

When I think of blue, I think of
An inky ink cartridge in a
Leaky pen.

When I think of blue, I think of
A small, playful and happy blue-tit
Like a child playing happily.

Anna Coles (9)
St Peter's Middle School, Old Windsor

RED IS . . .

Red is the colour of my future,
Red is the colour of red ink pens,
Swiftly going side to side making
Beautiful handwriting.
Red is the colour of blood,
Being pumped furiously around colossal
Bodies, using their mighty hearts.
Red is the colour of the spectacular
Sun, slowly and quietly going down in the sky.
Red is the colour of school jumpers,
Pouring rapidly into the great school.
Red is the colour of flowerpots with
Lovely red roses gently moving
In the soft breeze.
Red is the colour of pencil cases,
Bulging with writing things,
And gorgeous colouring things,
Red is the colour of my future!

Michael Irving (9)
St Peter's Middle School, Old Windsor

GREEN

See the grass swaying in the soft wind,
See the lizards, bright and green,
The frogs jumping into the pond,
Look at the sea crashing against the rocks,
See the lovely prickly stems,
Grasshoppers hopping here and there,
Out of the long green grass.
Look at all the apples falling off the trees,
Apples going into the pond.
I wonder how many apples there could be -
One, two, three.

Rebecca Chappell (9)
St Peter's Middle School, Old Windsor

GREEN

Green, green, green,
Comes out in the spring.
The grass glints with dew,
The daring green eyes shine like the sea,
The licking lizards lying in the green grass.
At the bottom of the sea,
The soppy, swaying seaweed.
The sound of the grasshopper's legs
Making a sound on
The green ground.
Sea shines with white lines.

Joanne Bradley (9)
St Peter's Middle School, Old Windsor

BLUE

The great shiver of my soul
Makes me feel cold.

Some waves make me warm,
And some make me feel freezing.

It makes me feel warm,
Like a summer sky.

It makes me feel like I'm floating in the air.
It feels like I'm asleep in the air.

It makes me think of a football team,
What am I?

Nicola Schwiezer (9)
St Peter's Middle School, Old Windsor

BLUE

As light as the sky,
As dark as the night,
As dark as the snow in the shade.
As cold as the freezing ice,
The sea, the lake and rain.
As light as the morning,
It makes me feel happy,
It reminds me of the swimming pool and ice,
I reminds me of the soft, gentle breeze,
Ice cubes, and rain.
Cold like a winter's day and ice-cream.
Cold like a glacier or a fast mountain stream.

Hannah Smiter (10)
St Peter's Middle School, Old Windsor

RED

Red is hot, hot as the sun,
Especially when the fire engines are out,
Down in the volcano the lava lays.

It's a fire, danger *stop* it now,
Something's floating up in space, is it the red planet?
No, it's a red suitcase.

Holly berries on a holly tree,
On Hallowe'en, vampires suck your blood,
The apples are yummy and so are the red hot peppers.

Red is *hot.*

Ben Canning (9)
St Peter's Middle School, Old Windsor

BLUE

Blue reminds me of the moving waves,
Blue feels cold and dull,
The splashing raindrops,
The silky flat lake,
The blue lake, hard and thin.
The blueberries dying and
Falling from the trees,
Leaving the colour behind.
People are stamping and
Squashing the berries,
And kicking them because they're unkind.

James Thomas (10)
St Peter's Middle School, Old Windsor

RED

Red is a hot colour,
Entering the sun,
Dropping rose petals on the floor.

It is like the colour of danger,
Stop and take care.

Glooping red-hot lava flows,
Red is a tubby called Po,
Every school jumper,
A rabbit called Thumper,
That is the colour red.

Carly Sansom (9)
St Peter's Middle School, Old Windsor

BLUE

My colour reminds me of the soft ice,
It looks like the dancing moon,
In the night sky,
It makes me think of the crashing
Waves in the sea.
It makes me feel like I am in an
Extremely cold ice cube.
I feel like I am drowning
In the deep ocean waves.
I am as still as a statue,
And I'm running against the rain.

Tom Sturley (9)
St Peter's Middle School, Old Windsor

SUNSHINE

Sunshine, sunshine,
Beautiful sunshine,
Sunshine shines in the summer time.

In the sunshine when the birds are singing,
When I'm in the paddling pool,
The bees come out and *ow!* The bee's stung me.

Sasha Peterson (8)
Sandy Lane Junior School

A WEIRD POEM

Today it is so boring listening to the teachers,
I'm sitting by a burning window, wondering what to do.
Then there is a creature in the tree, is it a purple dove,
Is it a pink and blue parrot, or a green and yellow fox?
Suddenly, the teacher asks me a sum - what's 9 x 999?
Uhhh? 8991?

Fiona Churchman (7)
Sandy Lane Junior School

SPRING POEM

Spring is when flowers grow and buds show.
Picture next spring twice as pretty.
Rabbits running around in the grass.
I listen to the singing birds in trees.
Nesting is going on and squirrels playing in the sun.
Growing in the garden.

Charlotte Oram (8)
Sandy Lane Junior School

MY FAVOURITE BOOK

In London town,
The bombs came down,
Four evacuees went to the country,
And for the first time saw a tree.

One boring day,
The children went to play,
Lucy quickly found a wardrobe,
With snow on the ground.

She met Mr Tumnus, the fawn,
With rather large horns.
He offered her a tea, she had some,
Little did she know the adventure
Had just begun.

Dale Nelson (8)
Sandy Lane Junior School

SPRINGTIME

Sunnier days,
Petals starting to come out,
Rainy days.
Insects starting to come out,
Nests are being built.
Green grass.
Trees starting to grow.
Insects coming out from hibernation.
Mother's Day.
Easter time.

Sam Viccars (7)
Sandy Lane Junior School

THE SUN

The sun is yellow, the sun is bright,
The sun is hot and pinkish.
When it sets it goes different colours,
The sun is very powerful.
The sun is mighty.
The sun burns like fire.
The sun is red and pinkish and yellow.
The sun is the strongest thing.
The sun makes plants look nice.
The sun can hurt your head.
The sun is incredible.
The sun is the biggest thing in the galaxy.
The sun is really hot, it makes your face sweat.
The sun is really hot, it makes you want to have
One hundred drinks a day.

Nathan Emmerson (8)
Sandy Lane Junior School

MY BROTHER

My brother is big,
My brother is older than me.
My brother's name is Allen.
My brother won't play with me.
My brother plays on his PlayStation.
My dad says that he thinks I play kiddie games.
But I think my dad is right,
He is too old to play my games.
But boys will be boys,
Because I don't think any boy,
Would want to play with a doll's house.

Sian Paes (8)
Sandy Lane Junior School

WHAT IF?

What if Nathan kicks my head off?
What if I do my work wrong?
What if I get grounded for a year?
What if nobody likes me?

What if I get kicked out of the football team?
What if I get knocked out?
What if I go on a roller-coaster?
What if I had a Tyrannosaurus Rex pet?

What if I had a plane crash?
What if the boat sinks?
What if I get punched?
What if I am ill?

Joe Fidler (8)
Sandy Lane Junior School

FRIENDS

Sometimes best friends are typical,
All except Shelby.
Shelby is the one for me, caring and kind.

My mum says we make a great pair,
We've just broken up now.
I play with Lauren.

Shelby and I have just made up,
We'll never ever break up,
What great fun,
I'm going to the disco with Shelby.

Rebecca Myles (8)
Sandy Lane Junior School

THE SUMMERTIME

The summertime
Is hot,
The summertime
Is fun,
The summertime
Is lovely,
There is nothing more
To say.
The summertime
Is . . .
The best time of the year.
In the summertime,
I can hear the birds,
In the summertime
I can hear the bees.
Everything is the best
In the summertime.

Rochelle Medford (7)
Sandy Lane Junior School

THE SEA

The sea is a lovely place,
Fishes swimming around, up and down.
As the people up above have their ice-creams,
Down in the deep, deep sea the fishes are having fun.

But up above, the children are playing on the sand,
Mums and Dads lying on their sunbeds.
Then the sun goes down, it's time to go.
It gets very dark at the beach,
But the children don't want to go.

Gemma Millard (8)
Sandy Lane Junior School

Portrait Of A Wolf

If I were an artist,
I'd paint a portrait
Of a wolf.

I'd do a proper job.
I'd borrow colours
From the world.

I'd use a dark, cold
Night for the wolf's
Eyes.

I'd use the bushes
From the forest to
Make the wolf's tail.

And I'd use the north
And south Arctics for
The wolf's bushy, white fur.

John Sherwood (10)
Sandy Lane Junior School

My Pony

I had a little pony,
Her name was Candy Lowe,
A golden palomino,
I really love her so.

I ride her in the snow,
I ride her in the rain,
What fun we have together,
I hope she never goes.

Shelby Lowe (7)
Sandy Lane Junior School

PETER PAN'S POEM

My favourite story is Peter Pan,
Who never grew up to be a man.
He came down to London to find some mates,
Then he went back to fight some pirates.

The leader of the pirates was Captain Hook,
He was a bad man in the book.
He wore a coat of red,
And wished to see Peter Pan dead.

But Peter and his friends were very brave,
Eventually they got Captain Hook to behave.
He fell in the water and was chased mile after mile,
By a big fat tick-tocking crocodile.

Daniel Rutter (7)
Sandy Lane Junior School

MY SCHOOL POEM

At school, teachers teaching children writing on books,
It's assembly and my friend has been naughty, he said it is me.
At playtime the air is fresh, what a lovely day for playing football,
It's an hour to lunchtime, I wish it was.
At last it's lunchtime, I'm coming in for lunch,
I wish I had a school lunch.
It's one o'clock, they blow the whistle,
And it's time to go in.
We do maths, that's fun.

James Mapp (7)
Sandy Lane Junior School

ICE PLAYGROUND

I walk into the playground,
I slip across the ground,
I look around,
It feels like I am the only one there.
I get blown across,
I fall down,
Ouch!
People in the playground,
Looking everywhere,
Some people get really cold,
I can hear the bird whistling,
The trees are dripping with cold ice drops,
We have a white playground.

Antony Evans (10)
Sandy Lane Junior School

SUMMER

Summer is playing on the field,
Summer is me playing football.
Summer is me with no top.
Summer is everyone getting hot.
Summer is ice cubes being made.
Summer is sports being played.
Summer is me getting the pool ready.
Summer is birds singing.
Summer is squirrels climbing.
Summer is lots of fun.

Daniel Viccars (9)
Sandy Lane Junior School

POLLUTION IN THE OCEAN

The beauty of the ocean,
Is hidden by toxic waste,
No one seems to care,
So which choice shall the creatures take?

'Our little ones are dying.' The injured creatures cry,
We must get rid of the toxic waste.
Though it takes more than just goodbye.

The bellowing, thundering pollution has taken over the sea,
it will take over a year to get rid of,
So now you really see!

It's more than just a crisp packet, or a can of Coke,
The ocean is now ruined and
There is nothing we can do.

So now on, be more careful,
And look after the sea, and everything
Will be all right,
And smiles you will see.

Emily Hawkes (9)
Sandy Lane Junior School

MY HOUSE

I love housework. I love my brother,
Now spring is round the corner.
We can play football with each other.
Mum is in the kitchen doing my tea,
Dad is watching television,
With Rex sitting on his knee,
Oh no! Mum's cooked peas!

Gary Adams (8)
Sandy Lane Junior School

OCEAN WORLD

Deep, deep down in the ocean,
Many creatures live.
There's a whale and lots of dolphins,
They like their glittering, sparkling, splashing home.

Deep, deep down in the ocean,
There's a load of beautiful, loving starfish, all calm and bright.
There's coral waving in the sea,
And excitement from the golden and wonderful fish.

Deep, deep down in the ocean,
There's a shimmering pearl which no human being knows about.
The dolphins guard, so no shark takes it.

Deep, deep down in the ocean,
There's some tropical jellyfish, all beautiful, but lazy.
The waves crash against the rocks,
While the sea is blue and green.
It then tingles back down.
It's so wide and deep,
So many creatures live in the
Ocean, ocean, ocean!

Michelle Riordan (9)
Sandy Lane Junior School

FIREWORKS

Fireworks in the sky.
All fireworks can fly.
Sometimes you can buy
Catherine wheels and sparklers
Everyone's happy.

Jay-Lee Dallas (9)
Sandy Lane Junior School

A PORTRAIT OF A PEACOCK

If I were an artist,
I'd paint the portrait,
Of a peacock.

To do a proper job,
I'd borrow the colours,
From the world.

I'd start with her tail,
I'd take all the colours of spring,
Starting with pink.

For her head,
I'd take the dark blue,
From the dull sky.

And her eyes
Will come from
A cave of darkness.

For her flapping wings,
Different shades of purple
Dotted on the paper.

I would gild her feet
From the gold
Of the sunshine.

Now for the best,
Her beak is the
Finest gold from the world.

Charlotte Dixon (10)
Sandy Lane Junior School

SNAKES AND LIZARDS

Deep in the jungle
Snakes and lizards,
Slither and crawl.
Snakes eat rats
Lizards chew mats.
Snakes lick Daniel
Lizards sit on Samuel
Lizard scores a goal
But snake stays back with Andy Cole.
Lizard gets kicked by a man
Snake is scoring for West Ham
Lizard goes to bed
And snake is squeezing a man's head.

Christopher Merton (9)
Sandy Lane Junior School

MY GUINEA PIG

My guinea pig is brown with a ginger tummy.
She runs around the garden like a maniac.
She has got three other guinea pigs to keep her company.
Their names are Posh, Scary, Baby and her name is Sporty.
They're like little lawnmowers eating the grass.
She lives in a very big hutch in our back garden.
They eat guinea pig food and other things.
Sporty dribbles a lot.

Grace Bryant (7)
Sandy Lane Junior School

MY CAT

Cats love to be stroked,
A fun day for a cat would be rolling in the sun.
They are very furry and friendly,
Sometimes they eat fish.

Elizabeth has a lovely cat,
A cat likes chasing mice.
The best thing for a cat would be sleeping *zzzzzz!*

Fish is my favourite food,
It's my cat's favourite food as well.
Sometimes she eats chicken,
Happy cats like playing.

Elizabeth Allen (8)
Sandy Lane Junior School

THE BEACH

When I go to the beach,
I see waves,
Gushing and splashing,
Seagulls overhead,
Flying over the sea.
I make sandcastles,
With the golden sand,
No clouds about,
People sunbathing on the sand,
The sun is red-hot,
With people sweating everywhere,
On the beach.

Ziggy Hughes (10)
Sandy Lane Junior School

IN THE OCEAN

In the ocean,
the glittering sea waves,
the multicoloured fish.

The shining sand
the seafish laying on
the seabed
the rough rocks.

The dark red crabs
and the black and white
whale.

And the shark's sharp teeth.

Limara Banks (8)
Sandy Lane Junior School

ON THE BEACH

I'm on a sandy beach,
Sitting on a bumpy rock,
The sea is smooth and gentle,
Boats bob up and down,
Sharks come out to hunt,
The sun is setting,
Air is cool,
Seagulls are going back to their nests,
As the sun goes down.

Daniel Reid (10)
Sandy Lane Junior School

IMAGINE

Imagine me,
As small as a bee,
Imagine a leech,
As big as a beach,
Imagine a flea,
As still as a tree,
Imagine a pig,
Trying to dig,
Imagine a whale,
Playing with a snail,
Imagine a lark,
Kissing a shark,
Imagine a rake,
Coiled up like a snake,
Imagine a crane,
Falling down a drain,
Imagine a hen,
Being used as a pen,
Imagine a girl,
Curled up in a shell!

Chantelle Napier (10)
Sandy Lane Junior School

THE WOLF

He's covered with fur all around to keep him warm at night.
He has sharp teeth like sticks to protect his baby.
When the hunters came, the little baby ran off.
Then the baby got shot.
The wolf started to get angry.
The wolf went to his dead baby.

Sadie Griffiths (8)
Sandy Lane Junior School

WET PLAY

Wet play is boring
Have to do drawing
Watch out the window
Watching the rain fall
Wet play is boring!

Wet play is boring
Stuck in the classroom
Sitting in my chair all break time
It is boring, wet play is!
Wet play is boring!

Wet play is boring
Rain is falling
Rain getting heavier
And heavier
Wet play is boring.

Cally Trotman (7)
Sandy Lane Junior School

MY FOOTBALL POEM

I kick the ball into the sky,
I kick my ball very high,
Up and up and up it goes,
Where will it land nobody knows.

It landed on a football pitch,
The goalkeeper missed it,
Hooray! I scored my first goal.

Connor Purches (7)
Sandy Lane Junior School

MY ROOM MONSTER

In my room that's full of gloom
There is a monster.
And at night he might . . .
Jump out at me you see
And give me a fright and maybe fight,
I don't want to go to sleep, I just want to peep,
I want to call Mum, but I'll just have to run,
I'm full of fear because nobody's here,
If I had my dad it wouldn't be so bad . . .
But I can't stand it at all I'll just have to call,
If the monster does attack me!

But now I'm older I think I'm getting bolder
I'm not scared of the monster
I think I'm getting stronger because I'm no longer afraid,
Though sometimes I fear that something is near
But really I'm not nearly as terrified,
And in the nights I don't get frights like I used to
It's not so bad as when I was a young lad,
Now I'm not scared of monsters!

Hudson Holt (9)
Sandy Lane Junior School

ME AND JAMIE

Me and Jamie are friends,
We sit next to each other,
We play together,
We like each other,
Me and Jamie are friends,
We go to each other's houses,
Me and Jamie.

Harry Skinner (8)
Sandy Lane Junior School

OCEAN WORLD

It's a hazy, lazy world down there,
where sharks and dolphins meet.

A whale swims by, a tingle
runs through the water.

I am the starfish so graceful,
so small.

The coral waves in the blue-green water,
dolphins play up, down and around.

Far, far beyond the shore I wait for
the fish to flash by.

Red, green, blue, yellow, silver, white,
golden sunlight peeping through the
curtains of rolling waves.

Dolphins jump high breaking the surface
what's this, a pearl of unusual size.

I love my ocean world
the world we created I think I'll stay forever.

We lay there glistening on the
sandy ocean bed.

Oh I love my ocean world
so much.

The waves are crashing,
churning up the surf and cooling the blue-green waters.

The soft and silky expression of the swimming
humpback whale.

Amy Cox (8)
Sandy Lane Junior School

BEAUTY OF THE OCEAN

Deep down the sea
down the blue lagoon
starfish shining.

Come into the octopus entrance
see the swimming, shimmering fish
see the dazzling . . . net.

Danger approaching
delicate fins breaking
colourful and delightful display
life endless . . . gone.

Jessica Johnson (9)
Sandy Lane Junior School

LISTENING

Can you hear
A car starting up
Someone sneezing
The motorbike?
Are you listening?
Can you hear?
A teacher shouting
Feet scrunching on the gravel
The murmur of children's voices
Are you listening?

David McQuitty (8)
Sandy Lane Junior School

SEASIDE

S mall sea creatures are nice
E ach time you go to the seaside it's great fun
A big crab bit me when I went for a paddle!
S ome people just go to the seaside for an ice-cream!
I hate it when we have to go home from the seaside!
D on't pour pollution into the sea because it kills the sea creatures
E veryone loves going to the seaside.

Elliott Clark (7)
Sandy Lane Junior School

THE LITTERBUG

Once there was a litterbug
A very bad litterbug,
He went around throwing rubbish,
He didn't care where.
All he did care about was being a litterbug.
If you have finished something,
You go and put it in a bin.

Danny Lalley (9)
Sandy Lane Junior School

AUTUMN

The wet grass flashing in the sun like emeralds set in a line
The hot sun making the logs shine
The sticks go brown and long
The aeroplanes so noisily passing
The wet, wet grass sticking out the ground like knives
The stones so smoothly carved.

Stewart Tibby (8)
Sandy Lane Junior School

ANIMALS IN DANGER

The elephant killed for his mighty tusk,
The gorilla for his holding hand,
Whales killed for their mighty black oil,
Sharks killed for a silly competition.

Help them live in peace in the lovely world God made us.

The poor pandas for transforming into a coat,
A rhino for his ivory horn,
Fuzzy bear fur for a rug,
The poor old tiger destined for the zoo.

Help them live in peace in the lovely world God made us.

Alex Harvey-Brown (9)
Sandy Lane Junior School

MY FRIEND

I have a friend, her name is Kelly,
she is a flying acrobat.

Me and Kelly are fighting flippers.

Me and Kelly are bowling
boulders and rolling rollers.

Me and Kelly are tired now
We shall sleep.

Zoë Hammond (8)
Sandy Lane Junior School

EXCUSES

My homework isn't here because . . .
My brother exploded it with a bomb,
My dog chewed it up,
My babysister was sick on it,
My mum spilt water on it,
My dad thought it was his book so he wrote in it,
My baby cousin used it for a football Miss,
I lost my pen,
My friend scribbled all over it,
My mum used it as greaseproof paper,
My sister burnt a hole in it for an experiment Miss,
My mum put her music on so I couldn't concentrate,
That's why my homework isn't in.

Toni Fidler (9)
Sandy Lane Junior School

MAN-MADE HELL

I keep away from the nets.
I dodge cans and other things.
There is no escape.
Can't give up I know I'm dying
But I won't give up.
I follow the humpback whales.
I can't go on but I must
Then again I am too weak.
I'm dying, I need to rest.

Martin Dixon (8)
Sandy Lane Junior School

WATERFALL

The waterfall is trickling,
Onto the smooth glassy water,
The silver water dazzles you,
When the sun shines down on it,
It's an extraordinary sight,
As the calm water shimmers.

Suddenly a massive gush of water blows down,
Boom! It hits the water,
The water charges towards the rocks,
Then the threatening water dies on the sharp rocks.

Everything goes silent,
The water goes all calm,
Everything is normal again.

Robert Knight (10)
Sandy Lane Junior School

WONDERING WHAT TO DO

I'm sitting in my chair.
I'm sitting in my chair.
Wondering what to do.
The teacher is talking.
I'm not listening.
I don't know what to do.
I'm fiddling with my pen.
I'm fiddling with my book.
I'm sitting in my chair.
Wondering what to do.

Siân Offen (8)
Sandy Lane Junior School

SOCCER

S occer is my favourite game ever.
O our team won the match.
C rowds were cheering for the winning team.
'C ome on' shouted the crowd.
E veryone was cheering for us.
'R ed card' shouted the referee.

Mathew Clacy (7)
Sandy Lane Junior School

SOCCER

S hoot a goal in the net and the crowd goes wild,
O h no! Another goal,
C rowd singing a lot today,
C ome on Ben get back up!
E veryone cheering for their team
R unning makes you get the ball.

Charlie Rennie (7)
Sandy Lane Junior School

SOCCER

S occer is a good sport,
O h yes we've scored a goal!
C an you hear the crowd cheering?
C oca-Cola Cup is the one we want,
E verybody is cheering for Chelsea,
R un, run you must score to win.

Elliott Rushforth (8)
Sandy Lane Junior School

THE GIANT SQUID

Humans are trying to get me,
I'm trying to swim,
Swim away as far as I can go.
I'm worried that they will harpoon me.
Then I saw a great black thing above the water.
It was black all over.
I was scared.
But I did not give up.
As I go through the silky water.
Fish swim away into the seaweed.
But I see the dark thing going away.
But I still have to be aware tomorrow.

Stephanie Reynolds (8)
Sandy Lane Junior School

PORTRAIT OF A DRAGON

If I was an artist,
I would do a portrait of a dragon,
I would use all the colours of the world,
His eyes would sparkle like diamonds,
His back as red as fire,
His spikes would be as green as pine trees,
His belly would wobble like jelly,
His fire would burn like the sun,
And his tail would be as blue as the sky,
That would be my portrait of a dragon.

Sam Myers (10)
Sandy Lane Junior School

THE ELEPHANT

It's time for me to go to bed,
I fall asleep and have a dream,
I've turned into an elephant,
I walk through the woods,
I hear gunshots.
I start to run,
I then meet up with some other animals.
Bang! Bang!
The people are getting nearer,
I slip on a leaf,
My friends hear the gun again,
Bang! They cover their eyes.
I've stopped breathing,
They cut off my tusks,
They cut off my feet,
They grab an axe and slice off my head,
They peel off my skin and hang up my skull,
That's the end of my dream,
I wake up and I'm shouting 'Help! Help!'
My mum comes up and calms me down,
I fall back to sleep and start again.

Laura Freeman (8)
Sandy Lane Junior School

MY DOG

My dog is annoying
Because he bites me
And I hate it
It is horrible.

Ben Waite (8)
Sandy Lane Junior School

THE SEVEN AGES OF A WOMAN

A young gift
So sweet and small
But then she starts to crawl
Before you know
She's a screaming schoolgirl
Grubby uniform, messy hair
But doesn't really seem to care
Grown up now
Tangled heart all of a flutter
It melts just like a pound of butter
Got a job working now
Goes down the pub with her pal
A brand new mother,
Starts to smother her little kid
Standing small
Always leaning against the wall
Starts to talk of those good old days
Then she passes to a better place.

Tamsin Munday (11)
Sandy Lane Junior School

THE TIGER

Using my fur for fur coats.
Now they're coming after me.
He's getting nearer to me nearer, nearer.
Nearly got me, I ran away.
Then he shot me.
My backbone was broken.
I was in great pain and agony.

Daniel Cartledge (9)
Sandy Lane Junior School

SEVEN AGES OF WOMAN

Once I was a baby all cute and small
Then I was a schoolgirl
Big and tall
By the time I was a teenager
I was six feet tall
Then I was a student
Not at school
Then I was a mother
Waiting in the hall
Then I was a manager
Of a swimming pool
When I was a grandmother
I was all lonely and sad
And then one day I went mad.

Hayley Blackall (11)
Sandy Lane Junior School

GREAT WHITE SHARK

Great white shark in the sea
Oh no the hunter's after me!
The hunter fires a harpoon,
It rockets into the water.
I dodge the poisonous needle.
I can't go much further.
It's hit me, I can feel it!
The blood is gushing out.
Flesh is peeling off.
I can feel my life ending.

Matthew Wears (8)
Sandy Lane Junior School

THE KILLER WHALE

I'm swimming through the ocean deep,
I'm scared as scared as can be!
Some hunters are coming,
And I don't know if they'll eat me!
They may use me for dog meat,
They may use me for food,
But they're not going to get me,
If I get away first.

I'm swimming through the ocean deep,
I'm swimming faster and faster,
The big, black beast is closer now!
Here comes another harpoon,
It's missed me this time
But next time I'm sure it will get me!

I'm swimming through the ocean deep,
My baby's on my back now.
The spear's sharp point missed me again,
I think I'm too good for the hunters,
I'm glad they've given up now
But I have to be aware for tomorrow.

Caroline Land (8)
Sandy Lane Junior School

MY FRIEND

My friend has a big dog.
It had puppies.
One of them is called Dipstick.
It is so sweet.

Alexander Halfacre (7)
Sandy Lane Junior School

THE EARTH AND BEYOND

Up high past the clouds the colour of vanilla ice-cream,
Beyond the glittering stars,
Lives a different world full of mysterious creatures,
Tanaka a small village filled with luxury,
Tropical trees filled with money,
Beds which float upon this village,
In the steaming hot air,
And plants the colour of candyfloss,
Animals that aren't on Earth like beautiful unicorns live here,
Which may come on Earth in another life,
Walnut whip bushes are here,
And delicious chocolate bubblegum drinks,
The villagers talk a muddled up language,
And are very friendly citizens,
Their hair is like spaghetti,
Their eyes are meatballs,
And their legs are made of string,
As you walk upon this village the weather seems a little
Strange, it's raining sun!

Danielle Metcalfe (11)
Sandy Lane Junior School

THE LITTER

Why do people drop litter?
Why don't people put litter in the bin?
Why don't people pick litter up?
Why do they leave it?
Why do bad people drop all their rubbish?
Why do good people put their rubbish in the bin?

Sam Whiting (9)
Sandy Lane Junior School

SEVEN AGES OF WOMAN

Once you're a baby
Next you're a schoolgirl
Seven ages of woman
Now you're a teenager
Next you're a single woman
Seven ages of woman.
Now you're a manager
Now you're a woman
Now you're getting old
You're a grandmother
You can't believe your eyes
Seven ages of woman
You're dying
Your family upset
Seven ages of woman
You have died,
What's next?
God, time got quick!

Zoe Booton (10)
Sandy Lane Junior School

GREAT WHITE WHALE

The great white whale swimming in the sea,
Oh no, a harpoon's chasing me.
I swim and swim, it's got my tail.
Oh no, I'm going down.
I try and get it off my tail,
But I go down,
I go to the bottom of the sea,
My tail hurts, I cannot swim.

Aaron Booton (8)
Sandy Lane Junior School

THE GREEN GLASSY WATERFALL

The green glassy waterfall,
Crashing from the sky,
Spraying grey-green water at me,
From the dark rocks up high.

Blue bubbling water roaring,
A white wonderful sight,
The sparkling dazzle of water,
As it rushes down with all its might.

Smashing silver droplets,
Falling down from the sky,
A shimmer of whirling crystals,
As down it does fly.

Alexandra Land (10)
Sandy Lane Junior School

BIRDS IN THEIR LIFE

A sparrow shoots like
an arrow flying around.
A bluetit shooting to
its nest with some food
in its mouth.
A yellow-headed bird
is flying with its nice colour.
An owl is scooping
for some field mice.
An eagle is flying in
circle by circle.

Mark Poole (11)
Sandy Lane Junior School

WHEN I GROW UP!

When I grow up!
I would like to be
A singer in a glimmery dress
Wearing lovely high heels in bright colours.

When I grow up!
I would like to be
A poet saying my favourite poem
Yes, that's what I will do.

When I grow up!
I would like to be
A queen with a crown
Which shimmers in the dark.

When I grow up!
I would like to be
A person who I've been all my life
Which is *me!*

Kelly Stockinger (7)
Sandy Lane Junior School

SOCCER

S occer is great!
O h no! The other team has scored,
C an you hear the crowd roar?
C an you hear the crowd sing?
E veryone is cheering for Man U,
R un with the ball and score.

Declan Cronin (7)
Sandy Lane Junior School

THE HAIRY, SCARY MONSTER!

There's a hairy, scary monster who likes my smelly socks,
My toys are hidden somewhere and I think they're in a box.
He rattles around and takes all my books and now I've had enough.
So I shouted out
'Hey monster, give me back my stuff.
You've eaten up my homework and hid my pairs of shoes,
I can't find them anywhere at least give me some clues.
But if I got rid of you, then I'd have to get the broom.
After all, I know you clean up this room.
So if you don't eat me or grab me in the night
You may have some peace and I won't have a fright.'

Christen Gaskin (10)
Sandy Lane Junior School

SPRINGTIME

S pring is fun, let's have a run
P is the second letter that is better.
R is for run, let's have fun
I have a sister I don't want to kiss her
N ests in trees and lots of bees
G reen grass growing, let's get going
T rees are growing, I am growing
I n the sun birds have fun
M y name is Jamie and it rhymes with baby
E nd is near, do not fear.

Jamie Harper (8)
Sandy Lane Junior School

MONSTER UNDER MY BED

Monster under my bed,
Monster under my bed,
He told me his name was Ted.

I gotta keep away from that monster
Gotta keep away right now,
Some how.

He's as smelly as a welly,
And he's got a big round belly,
Monster under my bed.

Matthew Blackall (10)
Sandy Lane Junior School

THE DESERTED HOUSE

Old creaking floorboards
Cobwebs on the ceiling
Small smashed window
No electricity
Aghh!
Ghosts singing
Bats on the ceiling
Yuk!

Simon Baker (11)
Sandy Lane Junior School

KATYA'S STORY

Elegant, silky, full of cat-like grace,
Better than most of the human race,
Eyes of emerald disdainfully gleam,
Rough pink tongue licks up her cream,
Curled up in a chair she appears to be asleep,
Yet look between the half-shut eyes, still the emeralds peep,
Delicate whiskers sense the air,
Small pink nose sniffs here and there,
Tiny claws and silky paws all belong to her,
Beautiful satin-like black, brown-white fur,
Perfect loveliness, all hers by night
What an example to those who rush, scream and fight,
A creature as simple and beautiful as that,
Katya a wonderful mysterious cat.

Rebecca Hawkes (11)
Sandy Lane Junior School

AUTUMN

We like autumn.
The wind is blowing
Nice and fresh.
The trees are swaying about.
Sweet wind
Is cloudy and windy too.
The rain is falling
On the ground.
Squirrels going back to hibernation.

Dominic Halfacre (8)
Sandy Lane Junior School

IF I WAS AN ARTIST

If I was an artist,
I would paint a picture,
Of a pretty parrot,

For its shiny beak,
I'd take a petal,
Of a gleaming marigold,

For its bright eyes,
I would take,
A lovely orange topaz,

For its feathers,
All soft and colourful,
I'd take strips of the clouds,

For the green,
All cool and nice,
I'd take a forest green,

For the red,
As fierce as fire,
I'd take a ruby,

For the blue,
I'd take the wavy sea,
Shining in the sun,

I've got the parrot,
In my mind,
I'll keep it there forever.

Victoria Fabron (9)
Sandy Lane Junior School

THE WATERFALL

The glass-like water drifts slowly,
then faster and faster,
as it approaches a plunging fall.

Echoing thunder's louder and closer,
slapping algae covered rocks,
grasping everything, don't want to go plunging off the edge.

Level and straight, level and straight then . . . down!
Tumbling crystals dazzling in dance,
drizzling, diving, thundering clash.

Slushing as it ends its fall
a circling wave drifting to the edge,
with a white-tipped frothy curl.

The glass-like water drifts slowly and calm,
then steady and paced,
as it has ended its plunging fall.

Jacqui Ross (11)
Sandy Lane Junior School

SCHOOL

School is boring, teachers nagging
I rock on my chair,
Then the teacher says 'Informal warning
Come and sit on the mat'
You are uncomfortable
You're not allowed to fiddle,
You have to stay still
Until they set you some work.

Sophie Hamlin (7)
Sandy Lane Junior School

SCOTLAND

Scotland is a very chilly place
Especially at
Winter
How the wind blows
Past your face,
And we mustn't forget
The little mites.

England is very different
Cars *zoom!*
Past you,
We're living in England
And I wish I was back,
Back in Scotland
Now.

Jamie Bunting (8)
Sandy Lane Junior School

MY HOBBY

I like rugby
Because it's fun
I like the shape of the ball
Because it's funny
I like rugby
Because I love to tackle people down
When the ref says offside
I give him a frown.

Rhys Mills (8)
Sandy Lane Junior School

WHAT IF . . .

What if I saw an alien dancing in the road?
What if the alien turned into a toad?
What if my dog ate a frog?
What if the frog danced with my dog?
What if our car blew up the driveway?
What if my cat did?
What if I fell off my bike?
What if my friend turned into a werewolf when the moon is full?
What if I get food poisoning?
What if I get murdered?
What if Chelsea lost their match?
What if Man U win?
What if it's a draw?

Lee Poole (11)
Sandy Lane Junior School

WATERFALL

Roaring as the water flows frantically over the edge
The foamy froth at the bottom bubbling and swirling
Like a tap that never turns off.
Sparkling when the sun reflects off the wet shiny rocks.
Freezing cold like the Atlantic wind.
Swaying boisterously from side to side smashing against
                                         the muddy rocks.

The water drizzling through a crack in the rocks
Running down the bumpy face.

Alex Lowe (10)
Sandy Lane Junior School

MILLENNIUM

Millennium, millennium,
How the world is going to change
The Millennium Bug is a terrible thing.

Millennium, millennium,
The sun is so old,
Just floating in the sky,
The moon as well.

The millenniums of the past,
And the future's to come,
To the world.

Will David Beckham
Be in the next world cup,
Or will he get sent off again?

Jake Roberts (9)
Sandy Lane Junior School

FIGHT

Fight is bad
People fighting, people dying
Mums and dads crying
Veterans praying
Saying they will come back
Or will they not?
Just let me know
And please hurry up
Fight.

Jamie Sweetzer (11)
Sandy Lane Junior School

LAKESIDE

Walking through the woods at night,
I always had a great big fright,
Whoo, boo, slash, bash,
I always went with someone else,
Or else I would be scared.

The mountains were tall and fat,
Very hard to walk up, but really fun to walk down,
The view from the top was wonderful,
Magnificent,
The green land below you and the animals below you,
When you walk down in the dark,
The river ripples down.

The river's ripples were crystal clear,
The ducks and swans swimming fast,
The water sometimes rough, sometimes soft,
The river made a lot of noise,
And it made it scary at night.

Emma Dixon (10)
Sandy Lane Junior School

EVACUEE

Line in line all the children stand hand in hand,
I am scared I will be taken away, away from my family,
I will go to a horrible house like I have before,
But I ran, I ran back home and knocked on my door,
I hugged my mum and dad and my little baby John,
My mum promised I would see her up in heaven,
We will go and be together forever and ever.

Kimberley Sage (11)
Sandy Lane Junior School

IMAGINE, IMAGINE

Imagine a slug, as small as a bug,
Imagine a cat, as flat as a mat,
Imagine a goose, as big as a moose,
Imagine a fox, as big as an ox,
Imagine a bear, as fast as a hare,
Imagine the Earth, as small as a smurf,
Imagine the classroom, as small as a bathroom,
Imagine a welly, as tasty as jelly,
Imagine a frog, as wide as a log,
Imagine a flood, as red as blood,
Imagine a hen, as big as Big Ben,
Imagine me, as small as a pea.
Imagine, just imagine.

Megan Warman (10)
Sandy Lane Junior School

AT THE BEACH

It's a warm sunny day at the beach,
The shimmering sun shines on my body.
I see the seagulls flying up high.
The sparkling sea is moving calmly.
I smell the salty air,
The slimy seaweed moves with the sea.

I feel the water against my legs,
I see a ship drift by.
The gritty sand sticks to my hand,
My wonderful day at the beach.

Natasha Singh (10)
Sandy Lane Junior School

NESSY

If I was an artist
I'd paint the portrait
of nessy.

To do a proper job
I'd borrow colours
from the world.

For starters I would
make his skin out of
the leaves from many silky trees.

His spikes would be
created by all the
fur trees in the world.

But his eyes would
have to be the ocean
sea.

His sharp teeth would
be made out of all the
deadly swords.

Last but not least,
his webbed feet made
from cobwebs to silk his
feet together.

Graham Newell (10)
Sandy Lane Junior School

THE MOST FANTASTIC SANDWICH I EVER ATE

The most fantastic sandwich I ever ate was made
by an old disgusting witch,
With a grand house which was most scarily haunted,
She added cooked adder, ants, spiders, bugs, even a bit of
witch's tongue to the sandwich,
She took long as she kept cackling but it was worth the wait,
As I bit into it I heard the crunch of snails, *mmm!*

The second bite tasted like chicken but there were
some worms in it so you would expect that,
And my third,
I can't describe,
It was so acceptable, scrumptious,
The slimy slugs melted into my watering mouth,
It was so moreish I wanted more rotten slugs but no,
Also in that bite I tasted the witch's tongue
with an ant carrying it, *mmm.*

On my last bite, the fourth bite,
I could taste the blood leaking out of the spiders
and cooked adder, scrummy,
And the stale bread mixed in well,
Then it was gone but I can tell you this, it was lovely.

William Croxford (10)
Sandy Lane Junior School

JAWS

The boat sped through the water,
With harpoons laid on deck.
One goes flying through the air,
And hits a great white's neck.

It thrashes out like mad,
Then takes his final breath.
He flops down to the seabed,
A pile of rotting flesh.

Rhys Bevan (9)
Sandy Lane Junior School

EARTH AND BEYOND

This glittering sky,
Way up high is like a spray of white paint.
The planets are like big bouncy balls,
That echoes when you call.

I bounce to and fro,
And all I see is a fluttering bee,
Flying above me.

As I follow the bee,
I see a strange tree.
It looked dark and gloomy
But chocolate dripped, dripped on me.

A bird with a tail,
Could it be?
Then suddenly the blue wings appeared on me,
I flew through red trees, mountains and streams,
Of peas.

A flash of lightning in a galaxy,
I have returned home now I can see,
A blue sky and my bed beside me.

Sarah Taylor (11)
Sandy Lane Junior School

IMAGINE

Imagine me
As small as a bean

Imagine a flea
As big as a tree

Imagine a flower
As tall as a tower

Imagine a cat
In a shape of a hat

Imagine a bean
Bark like a dog

Imagine a tree
As noisy as a bean

Imagine a house
The same size as me

Imagine a flea as
Fat as me.

Danny Bungay (9)
Sandy Lane Junior School

FRIENDS

I have lots of these
They are always there for me
I can always trust them.
What are they?

Friends.

Nikki Perry (8)
Sandy Lane Junior School

IMAGINE

Imagine a bee,
As long as me.
Imagine a dog,
As small as a frog.
Imagine a road,
As short as a toad.
Imagine a bat,
As long as a hat.
Imagine a goat,
As wide as a boat.
Imagine a mouse,
As large as a house.
Imagine the moon,
As little as a spoon.
Imagine a bun,
As bright as the sun.
Imagine a hook,
As big as a book.
Imagine me,
As tiny as a flea.

Charlotte Knibbs (9)
Sandy Lane Junior School

SOCCER

S occer is my favourite thing
O ver the weekend I played soccer.
C ome over to play soccer.
C heer for soccer.
E njoy the game.
R unning around the pitch.

Samuel Hughes (7)
Sandy Lane Junior School

BEST FRIENDS

They're fun,
They're fast,
They're wild,
They're free,
There's a best friend for you and one for me,
Charlotte,
Rebecca,
Alex and Erin,
They're my top four best friends now,
We play,
We laugh and
We run,
We muck around in the sun,
I hope we never fall out again,
Friends,
Friends,
Oh dear me, they ran away.

Hannah Myers (10)
Sandy Lane Junior School

WEATHER

Monday, crisp, sparkling, patterned, snowflakes fall,
Tuesday, squelch, squelch, muddy grass,
Wednesday, crunchy, munchy frost,
Thursday, splash, splash, splashing puddles,
Friday, windy, twisty gales pull trees down,
Saturday, bang, whoosh, crash, thunderstorm coming,
Sunday, sun, shining bright.

Megan Holgate (8)
Sandy Lane Junior School

THE WATERFALL

As my sister and I walk through the muddy wood
I hear a sound,
The crashing waves falling to the ground,
The dazzling grey and silver rocks up high in the air,
As I gaze, it is beautiful up there.

The trickling water and white waves as it foams,
Then the fall to all the stones,
Back to the flowing stream,
Then suddenly I hear a scream,
I turn round to see my sister standing there,
With lots of mud in her hair,
The water is all silent, even the fall,
What do I like best?
Well, it all!

Emily Bryant (11)
Sandy Lane Junior School

FRIENDS

Friends are very good to have
Rainy days we play inside
I like friends to play with
Even if we argue we still like each other
Never ever have a fight
Don't ever treat friends badly
Sometimes we break up but we always make friends again
We play together every day.

Ben Knight (8)
Sandy Lane Junior School

IMAGINE

Imagine a dog as big as a log.
Imagine a bee as big as me.
Imagine a rat as big as a cat.
Imagine a cat as big as a mat.
Imagine a whale as small as a snail.
Imagine a flower being sour.
Imagine a frog as big as a dog.

Joanna Martin (11)
Sandy Lane Junior School

SPRING

S pring is a time when flowers come out,
P eople play in the fields in spring,
R unning on Sports Day, day after day,
I am playing with my friends and family,
N ice time with all of my friends,
G ames again, Sports Day, I win!

Kandice Roberts (7)
Sandy Lane Junior School

SPRING

S pring is a good time to play with your friends,
P laying outside on your bike
R unning outside with friends,
I like looking at the daffodils,
N ice flowers are growing,
G reen buds are shooting.

Alexander Richards (8)
Sandy Lane Junior School

THE LIGHT FOREST

As I sit in the forest,
The cool breeze rustling my hair
The yellow sunbeams shining through the shimmering forest.

A deer leaping through the glistening, glimmering forest
The smell of pine rushing to my nose
Willow, oak, fern, holly are surrounding the forest.

Sunlight is catching part of the green leaves
Squirrels are collecting the green leaves
Sunny berries blue, red, black . . .

The rain starts to fall
A rainbow filling the blue sky
I can hear the rain on the leaves pitter, patter, pitter, patter . . .

Clara Ramsdale (9)
Sandy Lane Junior School

I SEE

I see children playing in the snow.
I see icicles forming on the gutters.
I see fog appearing in my sight.
I see the cold, the bitter cold.
I'm sliding on the silver ice.
There are mystical figures in the fog.
I see figures running, running towards me.
What is it?
It's coming towards me.
It's just my friend.

Luke Metcalfe (9)
Sandy Lane Junior School

IMAGINE

Imagine a spider,
As fierce as a tiger.
Imagine a dog,
As green as a frog.
Imagine a flea,
As tall as a tree.
Imagine a flower,
As tall as a tower.
Imagine a horse,
As long as a course.
Imagine a coat,
As thin as a rope.
Imagine a bee,
As tall as me.

Chelsea Henderson (10)
Sandy Lane Junior School

IMAGINE

Imagine a mat as big as a cat.
Imagine a goat as huge as a boat.
Imagine a house as small as a mouse.
Imagine a quail as large as a whale.
Imagine a goose as big as a moose.
Imagine a rat as large as a bat.
Imagine a lawn as small as a thorn.
Imagine a pot as big as a cot.
Imagine a land as tiny as a band.
Imagine the world as small as a swirl!

Emma Shoubridge (11)
Sandy Lane Junior School

I THOUGHT . . .

When I was little I thought . . .
There was a big, ugly monster under my bed.
I thought it would pull me under the bed,
And gobble me up.
I thought it was green, slimy with big lumpy eyes.
But I was younger then, now I think,
There is not a big, ugly monster under my bed.
I don't think it would pull me under the bed.
I don't think it would gobble me up.
I don't think it is green, slimy with big lumpy eyes.
Why did I think there was a monster under my bed?

Emma Lobar (10)
Sandy Lane Junior School

MY FAVOURITE ANIMALS

One white whale waiting,
Two terrapins thrash through thistles,
Three thrush try tasty treats,
Four fishes flap flimsy fins,
Five foxes forage forbidden food,
Six seals swimming so silently,
Seven squirrels seem so shy,
Eight apes attacking another animal,
Nine newts need new nests,
Ten tigers trample through trees.

Rebecca Comerford (10)
Sandy Lane Junior School

IMAGINE

Imagine me as small as a flea,
Imagine a flea swimming in tea,
Imagine tea 10 times bigger than the sea.

Imagine a frog as long as a log,
Imagine a log in the shape of a hog,
Imagine a hog playing with a fierce dog.

Imagine a whale as small as a snail,
Imagine a snail as tall as a male,
Imagine a male as furry as a fox's tail.

Carla Mackay (10)
Sandy Lane Junior School

IMAGINE

Imagine me
As a bee
Imagine Bracknell
As small as a centimetre
Imagine a mouse
As big as a house
Imagine a dictionary
As long as a blackboard
Imagine a shoe
As sticky as glue
Imagine a man
As tall as the 3M building.

Rebecca Halfacre (9)
Sandy Lane Junior School

There's A Monster Under The Sink

When I was little I used to think
A monster lived under the sink.
It was made of scraps of food
And when I saw it,
It used to move.
At night when I got my supper
I used to dread seeing this monster.
Every time I told my mum
She said your mind's just having fun.
It's still there and I still dread it,
But now I have a monster-catching kit!

Chloe Collins (10)
Sandy Lane Junior School

Up In The Mountain

Up in the mountains
very, very high,
a train awaits,
for people to say,
let's go on that tram
to see the beautiful
sight of the town
and the lovely breeze
upon the mountain.

Leisha-Louise Hann (10)
Sandy Lane Junior School

ON A MOUNTAIN

I'm sitting on a mountain,
Reflecting on my life,
How I learned to walk,
How to fly a kite.
It's very peaceful,
Though it's very cold,
The sun still shines on,
The sun is very old.

I'm sitting on a mountain,
Birds flying high,
Squeaking above,
In the cloudy sky.
The wind whistles in my hair,
The snow crunches in my hand,
It is so beautiful here,
I can't think of a more wonderful land.

Emma Pugh (10)
Sandy Lane Junior School

SNOWY

I come up the snowy steps
Snow is everywhere
The playground has ice-cold snow
I skid in the mushy ground
I fall on my face
My face feels so cold
As I get the snow off my face it is nice to go in
It is nice and warm inside.

Sam Dennis (10)
Sandy Lane Junior School

HUNGRY

I'm hungry,
Every day I hope it will rain.
I work all day
I'm tired.
I'm scared.
I'm going to fetch the water.
I'm hoping for dinner tonight.
My dad has just come home from work
He is ill.
My sister is getting thinner by the minute
She is only 3.

Vincenza Stevens (10)
Sandy Lane Junior School

CAN YOU HEAR

Can you hear the flower crying
when the rain hits the petal?
Can you hear your heart beating,
when it pumps blood around your body?
Can you hear your brain send messages,
round your body?
Can you hear your eyes,
when they blink?
Can you hear the trees chatting
when they sway in the wind?

David Nicholls (9)
Sandy Lane Junior School

MONSTER DREAMS

Monsters, monsters, creep up the stairs,
Nobody's listening and nobody cares . . . except me!

I wake up in a hot sweat,
Also feeling scared and wet.
Dark shadows lurk around,
Where the monsters are sure to be found.

Creak, creak, I'm sure there is a monster in my room.
I can't see it but I can hear its heavy breathing.

But where is it?
What is that noise?
Is it in the drawer rustling with my clothes?
Is it behind my cupboard door?
I'm sure I saw it move and the hinges are squeaking.
The door is creaking, the clock is ticking,
Outside leaves are rustling and owls are hooting,
Nasty shivers run down my spine,
Dark, gloomy shadows surround my bed,
I'm terrified, frightened, stiff and numb.
Suddenly I'm sitting up, I'm awake, for real.
Was it just a dream?

Monsters, monsters, creep up the stairs,
Nobody's listening and nobody cares . . . except me!

Emily Hanbury (10)
Sandy Lane Junior School

IF I WAS AN ARTIST

If I was an artist,
I would use the colours of nature to paint a tiger,
Its claws as dark as coal from a fire,
Its teeth as white as clouds,
Its stripes as dark as the night sky,
Its fur the colour of fire with yellow sparks,
Its head camouflaged in the colour of wheat in the field,
Its tail as stripy as you can imagine.

Stefan Goniszewski (10)
Sandy Lane Junior School

BULLY POEM

Bullies bully all the time!
Punch, kick, make you cry
Ouch! That hurt
Bully go away!
I hate you, we hate you every day
Bullies bully all the time!
Bullies punch, kick, make you cry
Call you names too, that hurts inside
But the worst thing they can do is bully you!

Kimberley Slark (9)
Shinfield St Mary's School

MILLENNIUM

The end of school, my favourite time,
because of the new millennium,
I wonder if the expected bug will affect the millennium.
Think of the food we will eat,
but think of all the poor people,
they might not think of the millennium.
Think of the Dome, the people who'll go there,
because of the millennium.
Christmas has gone, it's now New Year's Eve.
Soon the millennium.
It's 10 to 12, 10 minutes to go
for the millennium.
9 minutes, 8, 7, 6, 5, 4, 3, 2, 1.
Happy New Year!
All this fuss over one more year,
2,000 years since Jesus Christ was born.
The millennium.

Laura Dowling (10)
Shinfield St Mary's School

THE BULLY

The bully is big
The victim is small.
He hasn't got a friend at all
I hate him and he hates me.
He thinks I am no more than a little pea.
I say I hate you
He just sings 'I feel the same too.'

Michaela Lunnon (8)

-Shinfield St Mary's School

MILLENNIUM

Fantastic!
Exciting!
Super to you!
Stop to think about the starving,
And the homeless too,
What will they be doing on that eve?
They'll be starving,
And cold,
While we're partying on till dawn
It will feel like we've found heaven,
Within our death.
To them they'll have found hell,
Within their death.
What shall we do?
Nothing's enough!
Give up our parties?
No way!
Fantastic!
Exciting!
Super to you!
The millennium's for everyone!

Katharine Wright (10)
Shinfield St Mary's School

THE BULLY

Every time I go to school
Everybody bullies me.
They laugh at me like a fool
Teacher can't you see!

Neelum Ahmed (9)
Shinfield St Mary's School

BULLY WHY DON'T YOU GO HOME

The bully is back
Ready to smack
Ready to punch
Ready to whack!

He calls you names
Wrecks your games
He doesn't like you
He doesn't like your friends.

It's recess again
No punching
No whacking!
He won't wreck your games.

The bully is back
Ready to smack
Ready to punch
Ready to whack!

It's home time now
The bully's gone home
I'm so glad
I'm home with Dad.

I'm in bed, the bully is in bed
I wish I was in a wonderful world.

Danielle Weekes (9)
Shinfield St Mary's School

THE THING

The Thing is fat but very small,
Like a mouse.
It has eyes, emerald green
And its head and body are multicoloured
Just like a rainbow.
It has spikes all down its body,
As sharp as knives.
It lives in a tree trunk
And eats bread and mice.
It moves by jumping up and down,
With springs as legs,
So when you're walking in the woods
And see it . . .
Run
Because when it's mad, it's *very* mad!

Alex Bartkowiak (10)
Silchester House School

A TASMANIAN DEVIL

In a lush green jungle
There lived a massive humongous devil
It was so big
It could push over a ginormous tree
He spins so fast
He lifts up the grass
And nothing is left of the ground
He eats so quickly
He could eat an elephant in 2 seconds flat
He is a Tasmanian devil.

Tom Banks (10)
Silchester House School

THE THUNDERSTORM

The thunder was frightening and thundery.
It was quaking and brightening.
The dark, storm sky looked very scary.
Bashing and dashing, rushing and eddying.
Flashing turmoiling and toiling and boiling.
Threading and spreading, hissing and frizzing.
The dark clouds thundered.
The rain raged and roared.
The thunder tore and roared, rumbled and bundled.
It was flooding.
The rain made lots of gigantic puddles.
It sprayed everywhere.
It was dark then suddenly crash and *bash*!
The wind was strong, it was as though there was fighting.
Crash went the thunder, *bash* went the wind.
While I was all scared in bed.

Thomas Lees-Fitzgibbon (10)
Silchester House School

THE MINOTAUR

There once lived a minotaur
Who lived on the island of Crete
The minotaur's favourite dinner
Was tasty flesh and meat.

He was as big as a house
Yet still afraid of a mouse.
He said, 'I am so bored every day
I have nobody to have fun with or play.'

The next day a mouse went walking by
And saw the minotaur crying.
The mouse said, 'I'll use my strength'
And then the minotaur went flying!

William David Currie (8)
Silchester House School

MY DREAM

My uncle is a geographer
He told me lots of things in the world
The gorge, the desert, the mountains, the river
The trees, the animals, the seas of the world.

The lovely view of river Ganges
The huge desert of Sahara
The highest of the mountains in the world is
Eight thousand, eight hundred, forty eight metres.

I suddenly started my journey
I just could not control my mind but
I knew that there was happiness in the end
And I continued my endless journey.

Everybody thinks that I am strange
It seems to them that I only walk
Through distant landscapes, mysterious and strange
Towards the dream that I have made.

Yasumasa Kawata (11)
Sunningdale School

WHEN I WAS

When I was one,
Lots of grown-ups crowding round
Gurgle! Blurp! That sort of sound.

When I was five,
I was at my school
I learnt to swim in the pool.

When I was ten,
I was at a new school
The good thing was you are allowed to play pool.

When I was fifteen
More going out with your 'chum'
Not as much with your mum
Now I am thinking
Looking for a wife
Things have slowed down but I like my life.

Neville Galvin (9)
Sunningdale School

I AM BORED

I am bored, I am bored, I am having no fun
I am bored, I am bored, I am watching the sun.

I am bored, I am bored, I don't have a brain
I am bored, I am bored, it is going to rain.

I am bored, I am bored, there is nothing to eat
I am bored, I am bored, there is no one to meet.

Alexander Fraser (8)
Sunningdale School

THE HAUNTED HOUSE

I know a house near me
Which nobody wishes to see
As ghosts have haunted it
Since 1943.

People say the ghosts are green
I do not know, I've never seen
This is all a story
But the ghosts get the glory.

You can hear them screaming
But they are really singing
Tonight the house is glowing
Without anyone knowing.

Tom Malcolm (8)
Sunningdale School

THE MORNING

An owl,
Can scowl,
I look out of my window in the morning,
It is dawning,
I do not care,
Because my mother is out there.

I know a mouse,
That lives in our house,
We have scraps of food down there,
Our traps will be prepared,
That mouse is sly,
But we may catch a fly.

Henry Browne (9)
Sunningdale School

THE FIRE

Once there was a fire
It just started from a match;
It swept across buildings all in a flash
'Fire! Fire!' I shouted but nobody was awake, not even a liar.

Then somebody heard
And I said, 'Wake the people!'
But a voice came back, it was rather feeble,
'Help!' I could make out from the yelp.

I called the fire brigade
But it started to rain
Very much in vain!
'Hooray, hooray we're saved!'

William Bray (9)
Sunningdale School

OFF TO THE ZOO

We are off to the zoo
Off to see the animals
And enjoy the waterfalls
With all my friends and you!

The sun is shining high
The sky is clear and bright
Although teatime is nigh
But a long time till night.

Now the long day is ending
I like going to the zoo
We enjoyed laughing and playing
When we went to the zoo.

Aldwyn Boscawen (9)
Sunningdale School

SCHOOL

Why do you waste time at school
When you could be in a swimming pool?
Why do you have to use your pen
When you could be in your den?

Why do you have to look smart
And do art?
When you could be in the garden
Playing with your Aunt Cardigan.

Why at half past three
Do you get to see what is for tea?
These are good questions
That nobody can find solutions to.

Alexander Gordon (9)
Sunningdale School

THE SKY

The sky is bright,
With a bit of white,
It lets through light,
Not giving you a fright.

It hides the sun at night and noon,
So we can hear the birds cuckoo,
We always will respect the sky,
Towering over us so high.

The sun, the sky, the moon and stars,
Tell me when there's a party in Mars,
But luckily about the sky,
We will never say goodbye.

Harry Turner (9)
Sunningdale School

MY LITTLE TREE HOUSE

My little tree house up in the sky
At night we put beds in to lie,
In the morning we have some food,
My brother gets in such a big mood.

We had some friends for the night,
And we had a terrible fight,
Then we heard a creak,
The branch had broken, it was weak.

Suddenly I felt like I was flying,
Crash! We crashed and I was crying,
My mum and dad came out,
When they heard me shout.

Edward Walter (8)
Sunningdale School

A CLEVER CAT

There once was a cat called Kit
He went to the shop to buy a treat.
He took it home and said
'Mum, I want to go to bed.'

He woke up in the morning.
The sun was very warming.
The birds were all singing
And the bells were ringing.

The kitten went downstairs
To say good morning.
Then went back upstairs
To play shooting.

James Hawley (8)
Sunningdale School

SOS

If in an accident or distress
Easy call for SOS
Or even shoot up a flare
It will make the whole world stare.

When I'm in trouble and I'm at sea
The coastguard boat comes for me.
I know he came from the dark
To rescue me from a shark.

I think that he always is the best
Though I am to him a pest.
I am always in danger
But still he is my saviour.

Philipp Sjöström (10)
Sunningdale School

THE WEATHER

The weather is cold,
We will not scald,
The sky has many stars,
The road has many cars.

When the weather is sunny,
I'm very funny,
I have a toy pen,
I have some toy men.

The weather is stormy,
The sky is cloudy,
Twinkle, twinkle, little star,
Tell me where you are!

William Zhao (9)
Sunningdale School

BUSES

Buses go to and fro from place to place
But now and then they stop at bus stops
Buses very rarely have some space
But sometimes there's some extra room on top

Buses come in different shapes and sizes
Big ones, small ones and deckers double
Riding up high you view the landscape
And into gardens you can spy on couples.

Of horse riders, trotting, jumping the hedge
And then they're galloping down the street
With a kick they will reach the street edge
Soon you'll realise how boring buses are.

Christian Clogg (10)
Sunningdale School

THE SPEEDBOAT

There was a speedboat whizzing by,
Making spray go flying up high,
I saw the speedboat floating away,
Around the corner, into the bay.

The speedboat then came sailing back,
But something now it seemed to lack,
So I looked much closer then I saw,
That there was some water on the floor.

The speedboat kept on filling up,
Like an enormous plastic cup,
The crew jumped out and started to swim,
And so the tide brought them slowly in.

T Trenchard (10)
Sunningdale School

THE DAIRY FLIGHT

I got into the old plane
People said I was not sane.
The plane was a spitfire
An object I strongly admire.

I put the engine on
People said I'd soon be gone.
I checked everything was right
For the dairy flight.

Soon I was on my way
People said I'd soon decay.
The plane went very high
Soaring into the sky.

I crossed the English Channel
Looked at the instrument panel.
Saw the fuel was down
So I landed in a town.

I filled my tanks
And with many thanks.
With a big roaring sound
I departed from the ground.

I returned to Heathrow
Where many people go.
People said you look mucky
You are far too lucky.

Tristan Wood (11)
Sunningdale School

BUSES

Buses can be very fun,
As well they can be sulky.
It all depends if all the bends
Are nice or very bulky.

Buses are the only way
To travel very safely.
But if the driver's had a pint
It's like a flipping relay.

If you travel 22
The driver's nice and sober.
The only thing that worries you
Is you might be going to Dover.

I warn you now, I don't know how
To keep yourself awake.
Because many people before you
Have made the big mistake.

George Turner (11)
Sunningdale School

TIGERMOTH

A tigermoth to the left
A tigermoth to the right
And a tigermoth flying at midnight.

A tigermoth above
A tigermoth below
And a tigermoth flying too slow.

A tigermoth too high
A tigermoth too low
Plus a string of tigermoths flying to a show.

The running noise they make
While the Earth around rotates
And the sun begins to wake.

Frederick Barratt (11)
Sunningdale School

TRANSPORT

I could drive a car all day,
Speeding down the motorway.
Revving up clear and loud,
Feeling also very proud.

Why not take a bus I say,
'The only problem is you have to pay!'
All you have to do is sit,
And let the driver do his bit.

If you take an aeroplane,
You could even fly to Spain.
Going past the shiny stars,
Running past just like cars.

How about a holiday,
If it's hot in good old May.
But find a perfect transport link,
Because all the bad ones pollute a stink.

James Wemyss (11)
Sunningdale School

TRANSPORT

When going down the street,
A bicycle is easier than feet.
But when going downhill,
Your feet definitely aren't still.

I love my bicycle,
More than my dad's motorcycle.
See me going off jumps,
It is as bad as having mumps.

When biking in the rain,
My paintwork gets a smudgy stain.
When I get out the brush
I will make my bike smartly plush.

Mungo von Halle (9)
Sunningdale School

WEEDS

In the forest you can find big weeds,
Some attract bees
They are mostly green
And lots of them look very mean.

In the woods nasty weeds grow,
Some are as big as my brow,
Some are friendly like moss,
But not as cold as frost.

Some are dangerous like stinging nettles,
But not the rose petals,
Do not trip over the brambles
Don't step on them with sandals.

Benjamin Busk (9)
Sunningdale School

THE ZOO

At the zoo there is lots to do,
You see the animals black and blue.
Some live on land,
Some animals are big and grand.

Snakes make me shake.
The goose and the moose are my favourite animals.
Most of the monkeys climb on walls,
Some of the sea lions play with balls.

I saw an elephant,
And a hyena pant.
I saw a whale's tail,
Which looked like a sail.

Humphrey Atkinson (9)
Sunningdale School

THE JUNGLE MONKEY

The monkey swings from tree to tree
Not orang-utan nor chimpanzee
Can keep up with him
He's the top of the team

He's as light as a feather
He doesn't like rainy weather,
Flinging from branch to branch
He's faster than an avalanche

Quicker than a Boeing 737
He's tripping up on heaven
Would you believe it?
A dog could not achieve it.

James Balfour (10)
Sunningdale School

MILLENNIUM CELEBRATIONS

Bang the banger!
Snap the snapper!
Shoot the streamer!
Pull the cracker!

Whiz the whizzer!
Pop the popper!
Drink the Tango!
Dance the Congo!

Millennium:

Bug

Millennium Bug is a computer problem that has just occurred,
It's all to do with computer dates that have to be transferred.

Year

Another thousand years have passed; this century's come to an end
Time seems to have gone so fast and on it we depend.

Song

Millennium song is a song, sung by Robbie Williams
Everyone thinks it's so good - recommended by millions!

Dome

Millennium Dome is a building, built for the millennium
Where people from all around the world will hold their celebration.

Joseph Moore (10)
The Pines Junior School

THE MILLENNIUM IS HERE!

Bangers up, balloons fly high,
Parties are everywhere,
Millennium planes in the sky,
Crowds cheer, millennium's here.

The new year has set in,
All over the world the millennium's here,
Iceland, Antarctica and Romania,
That's right the millennium's here.

Dogs howl, cats miaow because the millennium's here,
Planes write in the sky the millennium's here,
The new year's brought it in,
Crowds only cheer once,
'The millennium's here!'

Kirstin Tricker (11)
The Pines Junior School

BLUE

Blue is the colour of the dark evening sky.
Blue is the colour of my literacy tray,
where my books lay.
Blue is the colour of my feathery pillows,
where my head rests at night.
Blue is the colour of my quilt covers,
that keep me warm at night.
Blue is the colour of windy waves at sea.

And blue is the colour of my pencil case,
where my pencils are kept safe.

Danielle Cooper (11)
The Pines Junior School

AUTUMN

Misty morning
    Golden leaves
        Soft fruits
            Around the trees

Misty morning
    Squirrels asleep
        Time to feast
            On autumn treats

Misty morning
    Spider webs
        Shining like pearls
            Among the threads.

Danielle Warner (11)
The Pines Junior School

A RIVER'S LIFE

Bubbling out of the spring,
The river skipping and hopping.
Dancing down the mountain,
Eroding her way to the green grass.
When she sees the town ahead,
She gradually gets slower.
Meandering quietly.
Depositing behind her.
She sees reservoirs taking her water.
Making her way to the sea.
Watching the trees go by,
Slowly and quietly, she dies away into the sea.

Louise Drewett (9)
Westende Junior School

A RIVER'S LIFE

Springing out from a source
trickling, jumping, running with joy.
Swerving, twizzling, falling, not far,
transporting rocks from field to field,
getting wider every minute.
Seeing houses go past fast,
twisting, turning, twitching,
travelling into flat ground.
Growing when it's gloomy,
shrinking when it's sunny.
Getting bigger, closer to the weir.
One last meander before the small drop,
falling, spraying, recovering again.
Nearing my old stages.
Slowly seeing the beauty of life
closing to my big rest
the end is in sight.

Fiona Spooner (9)
Westende Junior School

WIND

The wind is cold.
The wind is fearsome.
The wind is strong.
It goes on so long.

The wind can twist.
The wind can whirl.

It can pick up houses,
In parts of the world.

Joshua Swabey (7)
Westende Junior School

THOSE WERE THE DAYS

Those were the days
When I splashed on the rocks.
I used to skim along the pebbles.
'Having fun' was my motto, always jolly and lively.
Dodging all the fishes to finish the never-ending race.
I got older, depositing some of my stones.
Meandering, swerving, round the bend,
Slowing a little but still enjoying life.
And now, very old, hardly moving.
I cut corners, stop in ox-bow lakes,
Slowing completely.
I see the estuary, I'm coming to an end,
Coming to death, or maybe
A new beginning.

Joel Molloy (10)
Westende Junior School

MY TEACHER

I like my teacher, I think she is great!
She eats with her fingers and always comes to school late!
She sits down at the piano with her jumper the wrong way round,
Then plays a song with the most screechiest sound!
She eats so many chocolate bars they seem to come out of her ears!
Then she is sick for at least one thousand years!
And when we go to lunch the ice-cream's always eaten,
And when we play hockey she never gets beaten.
She comes into school with a smile on her face
But on Friday she frowns all over the place!
But if you chat you better watch out
Because our teacher's about!

Harriet Lawman (10)
Westende Junior School

My Birth To My Death

Springing up from the ground,
I started my birth
I was jumping and skipping with joy
Splashing and hopping as erosion starts
I love to play with the sharp and smooth stones.
When the weeds transport down, they tickle me.
Zooming *down, down, down, down.*

Now my life is slowing down but still active.
I glide into villages and farmland looking for jobs.
Bridges come and cover me up
But I miss them by going round and round.

Now I am very old and I glide ever so slowly.
I sleep a lot and then I enter the sea.

RIP.

Sarah Bullett (10)
Westende Junior School

Darkness

The lights go out when I'm asleep.
I wake up at midnight, scared and alone in the dark.
I can see outlines of teddies at the end of my bed.
I get out of bed and walk downstairs.
I can hear creaking and owls tooting.
Looking in the living room I see something move.
I feel scared and suspicious.
Specs of light shine through the window.
I creep upstairs, get in my bed and go to sleep.

Marc Pinnock (10)
Westende Junior School

IN THE DARK

The lights go out
But I'm still awake
I left my teddy out of bed
One leg out of the bed, it's cold
The other leg out of the bed, it's freezing
I step onto my rug
With tassels that look like fingers
And I walk across my floor, it creaked
Thank God it was only the floorboards
Shadows moving everywhere
I turn around there's a ghastly shadow there
So I twirl around again
Phew it was the reflection of the moon in my mirror
I can see a pair of hands sticking out of my drawers
What is it?
I reach for where I think the light is, it's not there
So I move up a bit, I've found it, I turn it on
I'm no longer in spook land
The pair of hands were gloves
And the teddy was on my bed.

Helen Jesson (9)
Westende Junior School

THE SAD COMPUTER

No one likes me at all.
They've never cleaned me once at all.
They just play me all day,
I wish I could just go away.
Away where nobody will see me,
Except just maybe one honeybee.

My eyes are in the screen,
So I could watch him play and scream.
My fingers are the keys,
So I could shake his hand and squeeze.
My body is where they feed me disks,
But I would rather have a bag of crisps.

Richard Putterford (10)
Westende Junior School

THE RIVER

He was created underground
But now he's born,
Running and skipping,
Splashing and splishing,
Waterfalls and plunge pools,
Playing with rocks and riverbanks.

Until he goes on holiday,
Towns, cities and far away.
Getting slow but still quite fast,
Under bridges for cars and trains,
People throwing stones and pebbles into him.

Now he's slowed down a lot,
Slow meanders left and right,
Nearing sea-heaven - bit by bit.
There he goes, goodbye river,
Goodbye forever.

Duncan Lock (9)
Westende Junior School

THE UNKNOWN LADY

As
she
skips on
eroding her way
she starts to play with
a pebble. Just alive and active
still at the young stage taking her time
to grow up and move on. As she swerves
round and meanders on her way, always playing,
no time to rest.

But now she's getting older, slower on her way,
passing all the farmland, towns and bridges, newborn
tributaries coming her way, she can feel she's nearly there,
the sea is getting closer and closer. Slower and slower as she is
nearly mature, at the old stage going to sleep.

She's asleep in an ox-bow lake, but just as she wakes up
and feels she is so close, the current is so slow as she cuts through
making ox-bow lakes hearing and smelling the sea, she sees the
end of her journey, the sea is in sight.

Goodbye land.

Katie Longhurst (9)
Westende Junior School

MY RIVER LIFE

I was splashing, skipping and diving around
I couldn't stop the fun.
And I'd only been born a few seconds
And it was so exciting.
I clashed against the rocks,
But now I am moving on.
I wasn't so playful
I go slowly around the meanders.
All I did was look
At towns and villages.
I was plain and boring
But time still moved on
I started to sleep, take rests.
My current was so slow.
My ox-bow lakes were still
I was by myself in silence
Finally I came to an end
I stopped and my
Life had
Finished.

Jade Merritt-Carpenter (9)
Westende Junior School

WIND

When it's windy I like to play and have my friends round to stay.
When the wind blows it sometimes flows but it always goes again.
I always know when the wind does blow and go.
I love the wind, do you?

Lucy Hamblin (8)
Westende Junior School

WATERFALL

As she
  splashes
   down and
    swims around
    she's scared
    of heights.
   She still
   likes
    going
     down
    and
    down
   and
  twisting
around
  she's never
   going to
    pause
     that's why
      she's
      a waterfall.

Simon Tetley (9)
Westende Junior School

WIND

The wind is
strong.
The wind is
long.
The wind is
cold.
The wind is
big.

The wind is
invisible.
The wind is
silent.
The wind is
high.
The wind is
weak.

Piers Boardman (8)
Westende Junior School

The Coral In The Sea

In the sea, dangers creep.
So it's not a good place to play hide and seek.
In the murky waters, green
A coral reef began to lean.
Next day it fell,
It crushed a shell.
Every little fish
Began to wish.
That the coral would grow
But no, it was too slow.
Don't start crying
Because they kept on trying.
And as if by magic
It just went click!
After summer with the sun
After winter with the snow
It began to grow.

Natasha Tompsett (10)
Westende Junior School

A River's Life

As I splash over rocks
Spraying water everywhere
Only just been born
Able to meander at top speed
Not knowing what's around the corner
Suddenly going fast, descending into a plunge pool,
Dazed I carry on.

But no, hold on,
Now I don't feel so playful
And still I go quite fast
I deposit and erode on either side
Then on the next meander I decrease my speed.

Now I'm on the last section of the journey
Very, very slowly I go round the corner
Past an ox-bow lake
Under a brick built bridge
As I get closer to my destiny
Round the next corner I see it . . .
The sea, and now I'll end my life.

Daniel Fenner (9)
Westende Junior School

Stages

Little bubbles drifting on the surface.
As a fresh start begins.
Wobbling, toddling along, as if it can't hold still.
Little splashes like tears,
Running along fast,
Flowing to a never-ending stop,
Growing but still on the go.

Getting a little bit slower,
Wider as it goes along,
Meandering, twisting, wanting to go a different way,
Now so worn out but still going along,
Carrying all his thoughts from when young,
Slowly struggling getting near the end.
Nearly there so many obstacles in his way but
Drifting along and fades away to sea, never to be seen again.

Carly Clark (9)
Westende Junior School

THE RIVER LADY

River Lady has just been born.
Skipping and dancing her way into a new life.
Playing with rocks and then dumping them
To start a new game.
As she crumbles away edges to make
A route for her journey.
Jumping across the sandy outlook
River Lady finds herself moving through
Meandering, trying to find her way.

She is getting older and now not so active.
She has come to her first town and she knows she must go on.
Tributaries been born, just like she once was
But time is passing, now no more games just
People using her as she gets wider.

Now slower, slower, she matures,
Observing her last sight and remembering memories.
And slowly she moves
Her way into the sea!

Lindsay Dier (9)
Westende Junior School

THE RIVER

He trickles, faster and faster,
Jumping, running, splashing and kicking.
The river frolicking, laughing, screaming and shouting.
He's playing with the rocks.
Crash! He dives over the waterfall and goes
Into a bend, he starts to slow down.
He goes in and out of the rocks, he starts to relax,
He quietens down. He slowly moves through the town,
Under the bridge.
He silently moves along winding his way through the meanders.
He eats into the banks and makes ox-bow lakes,
He climbs in and goes to sleep.
He is going to die . . .
But is he?

Thomas Hughes (10)
Westende Junior School

THE CAT FROM ROME

There was a posh cat from Rome
Who wanted a friendly home.
He hunted the street
For some fancy treats but
He ended up in a lot of foam.

Sean Noyes (10)
Westende Junior School

166

The Journey Of A River

The river leaping, dancing into life,
Whilst smelling the fresh mountain air,
And swishing round corners,
He is so lively now but soon he'll be quiet and slow,
Now he's halfway through his life and journey,
He's slowing down,
Every day getting closer to the sea,
Now he's moving very slowly,
So slowly that some of him sleeps in ox-bow lakes,
He can see the mouth of the sea,
He's getting excited,
Now he's entering the mouth of the sea,
At last the journey's over,
Into the wide open space forever and ever.

Jason Farrimond (10)
Westende Junior School

Darkness

I feel scared, creepy and even a bit startled.
I see an outline of something that looks more like a tree.
Suddenly I felt the wind cast up behind my cold back.
The road is silent, no sound to be heard.
The rain is getting heavier, I decide to go back inside.
The rain came down like thousands of hailstones
Falling from the pitch-black sky.

Andrew Marley (9)
Westende Junior School

HARVEST

Harvest is fun and happy
Think of animals, mice and rabbits
We give our money to poor people
We celebrate this happy day and we have a feast
We think of others with no money
We think of others with no food
Farmers collecting up their corn
Little flowers grow and grow
Sunset falls, summer's gone
Autumn's here again
Think of birds making nests
Horses eating hay
Squirrels burying nuts
Because it's harvest day.

Elizabeth McFetridge (10)
Westende Junior School

IF YOU WANT TO SEE A TIGER

If you want to see a tiger you must go to the spooky jungle.
I know a tiger who's living down there.
He's tough, he's rough, he's fierce, he's growly.
Yes if you really want to see a tiger, you must go to the spooky jungle.
Go down loudly and say come up, come up, come up, come up,
You weakling of the dead.
And don't hang around just don't jump out of your skin, just *run*!

Jamie Allwood (8)
William Gray Junior School

IF YOU WANT TO SEE A TIGER

If you want to see a tiger,
you must go into the gloomy
dark echo cave.

I know a tiger who's living
down there
he's mean, he's fat, he's smelly.

Yes if you really want to see a tiger
you must go into the gloomy dark echo cave.

Go down quietly to the cave and
say little tiger, little tiger, little tiger.

And up he'll rise
but don't just stand there
just run for your life!

Katharine May Hooper (8)
William Gray Junior School

IF YOU WANT TO SEE A TIGER

If you want to see a tiger you must go to the spooky jungle.
I know a tiger who's living down there.
He's big, bold, jumpy.
Yes, if you really want to see a tiger
You must say come on, go down the path and say come on.
If it sees you before you see him, run for your life.

Scott Smith (9)
William Gray Junior School

IF YOU WANT TO SEE A TIGER

If you want to see a tiger
You must go to a big black wood.

I know a tiger,
Who's living down there
He's fat, he's the king, he's silly.

Yes if you really want to see
A tiger, you must go to the big black wood.

Go down the big black wood and say
Tiger dada, tiger dada, tiger dada!

And he will get up and he will
See you first but you will say

'Run for your life!'

Michaela Masterman (8)
William Gray Junior School

IF YOU WANT TO SEE A TIGER

If you want to see a tiger
you must go to the crowded jungle.

I know a tiger who's living down there,
he's kind, he's mean, he's an ugly tiger.

Yes, if you really want to see a tiger
you must go to the crowded jungle.

Go down carefully and say

Tiger bad
Tiger bad
Tiger bad.

And up he'll come
but don't stick around
run for your life!

Hannah Knight (8)
William Gray Junior School

IF YOU WANT TO SEE A TIGER

If you want to see a tiger
you must go down to the long green grass

I know a tiger who's living down there
he's orange and black,
with a tail that goes whack!

Yes, if you really want to see a tiger
you must go down to the long green grass.

Go down to the grass and say
to the tiger 'Let's go and play'

And what have you done,
you've had good fun
but now it's time to run.

Lana Atkins (7)
William Gray Junior School

IF YOU WANT TO SEE A TIGER

If you want to see a tiger,
you must go down to the
muddy, gloomy zoo.

I know a tiger who's living down there.
He's big, he's stripy,
he's dangerous.

Yes, if you really want to see
a tiger, you must go down,
to the muddy, gloomy zoo.

Go down smoothly and say
tiger papa,
tiger papa,
tiger papa.

And up he'll come,
he might see you first,
so *run for your life!*

Ashleigh Bishop (8)
William Gray Junior School

IF YOU WANT TO SEE A TIGER

If you want to see a tiger
you must go down to the dark, gloomy
rainforest.

I know a tiger who's living down there
he's stripy, he's cuddly, he's bouncy
He's Tigger.
Yes if you really want to see a tiger
you must go down to the rainforest.

Go down quietly and say
Come out
Come out
Come out!

And he will come
out and say
bouncy, bouncy.

Beckie West (8)
William Gray Junior School

IF YOU WANT TO SEE A TIGER

If you want to see a tiger,
you must go to the
tropical rainforest out west.

I know a tiger who lives down there
he's stripy and big.

Yes if you really want to see a tiger
you must go to the tropical rainforest out west.

Go down through the dark trees and say

Come out,
come out,
come out.

And he will come,
but if he sees you first
run for your life!

Adam Ratcliffe (7)
William Gray Junior School

IF YOU WANT TO SEE A TIGER

If you want to see a tiger
you must go down to the
darkest, gloomiest, dampest
jungle.

I know a tiger
who's living down there
he's furry, he's fast
He's sneaky.

Yes if you really want
to see a tiger, you must
go down to the darkest,
gloomiest, dampest jungle.

Go down carefully and
say come on, come on,
come on.

And he will come all right
but when he comes, run!

Richard Barns (7)
William Gray Junior School

174

IF YOU WANT TO SEE A TIGER

If you want to see a tiger
you must go to the edge of
the Caribbean island.

I know a tiger
who's living down there,
he's strong,
he's big,
he's fierce.

Yes, if you really want to see a tiger
you must go down to the edge of the Caribbean island.

Go down slowly and say
Tiger dada
Tiger dada
Tiger dada.

And he'll look at you,
but don't stay,
run!

Nikki Lunnon (8)
William Gray Junior School